WWII Historic Battlefields

FROM THE
RIVIERA
TO THE
RHINE

US Sixth Army Group
August 1944–February 1945

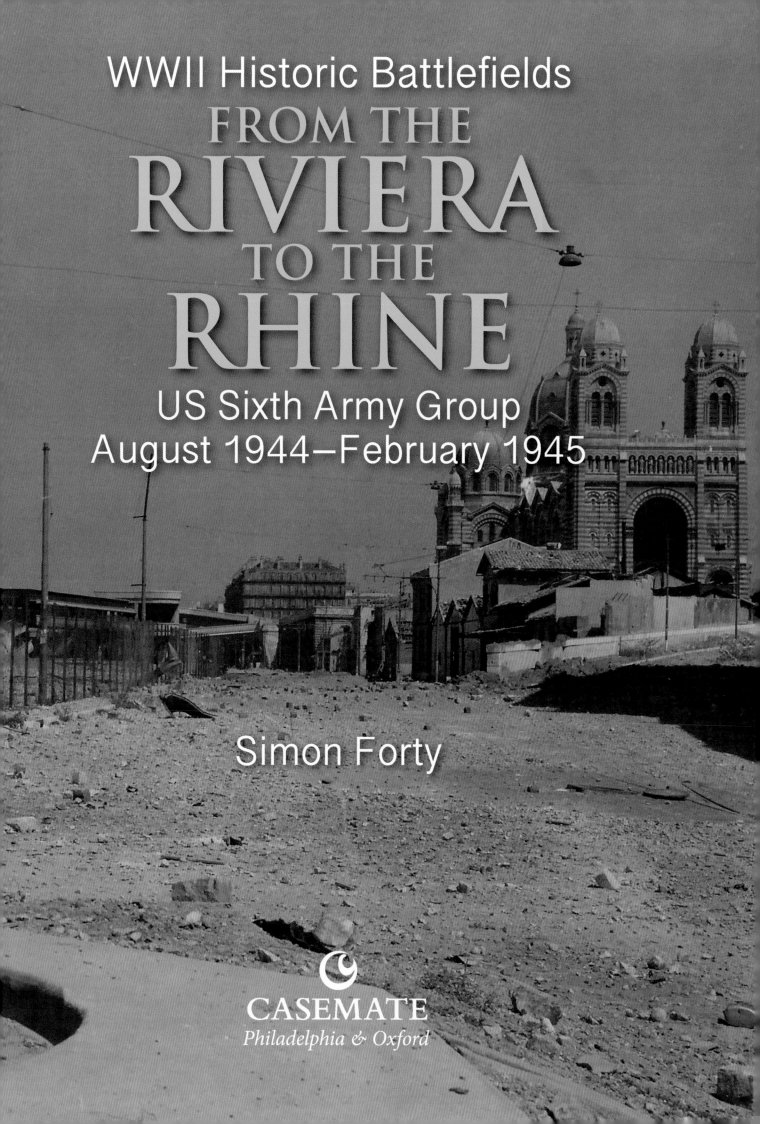

WWII Historic Battlefields

FROM THE
RIVIERA
TO THE
RHINE

US Sixth Army Group
August 1944–February 1945

Simon Forty

CASEMATE
Philadelphia & Oxford

Published in the United States of America
and Great Britain in 2018 by
CASEMATE PUBLISHERS
1950 Lawrence Road, Havertown,
PA 19083
and
The Old Music Hall, 106-108 Cowley
Road, Oxford, OX4 1JE

Copyright 2018 © Simon Forty

ISBN-13: 978-1-61200-623-9

Produced by Greene Media Ltd.,
34 Dean Street, Brighton BN1 3EG

Cataloging-in-publication data is
available from the Library of Congress
and the British Library.

10 9 8 7 6 5 4 3 2 1

Printed and bound in China

For a complete list of Casemate titles
please contact:

CASEMATE PUBLISHERS (US)
Telephone (610) 853-9131, Fax (610)
853-9146
E-mail:
casemate@casematepublishers.com

CASEMATE PUBLISHERS (UK)
Telephone (01865) 241249, Fax (01865)
794449
E-mail:
casemate-uk@casematepublishers.co.uk

Page 1: *US paratroopers on D-Day.*

Page 2–3: *A French APX R tank turret used as a pillbox to defend Marseille's harbor area. In front, at left the piers for liners; at right the Cathédrale Sainte-Marie-Majeure de Marseille.*

Below: *Mittelwihr was almost completely destroyed during the fighting around Colmar. Today it's on the "Route des Vins." The ladies are walking past a knocked out late-model Jagdpanzer IV/70.*

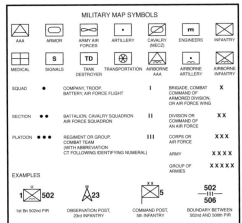

MILITARY MAP SYMBOLS

CONTENTS

INTRODUCTION

D-Day for Operation Dragoon was August 15, 1944. Originally—from August 1943—codenamed Anvil, its name was changed on August 1 to Dragoon. There are a number of reasons given for this: that the codename had been compromised or for security reasons—although everyone who was anyone, on both sides, in the Mediterranean theater knew an attack was imminent. The best story is that Churchill suggested it because he had been "dragooned" into accepting the operation—a play on words that fits well whether or not it is apocryphal.

This photograph shows US troops coming ashore on D-Day. In the background are the British LCI-133 and LCI-316. Built in the United States, these large infantry landing craft were armed with a 2pdr QF Mk VIII and three 20mm Oerlikons. They could carry 188 troops or 75 tons of cargo.

The opening paragraph of the Green Book sums up the campaign that started in the landings on the French Riviera in August 1944: "Although ultimately proving to be one of the more important Allied operations of World War II the invasion of southern France has also remained one of the most controversial. Most judged the enterprise solely on the basis of its effect on the two major Allied campaigns in western Europe, the invasion of northern France and the invasion of Italy. Supporters, mainly American, pointed out its vital assistance to the former, and detractors, mostly British, emphasized its pernicious influence on the latter."

That it was successful there can be little doubt: whether it was "important," provided "vital assistance," or had a "pernicious influence" is, perhaps, more debatable. The German forces in the south—what there were of them—were never completely trapped and annihilated. Denuded of its armor and its most effective troops sent north to combat the Normandy invasion, the static divisions, *Osttruppen*, and reserve divisions of German Nineteenth Army were badly mauled by the US and French armies on their way up the Rhône valley, but many troops were able to escape and fight again. The south of France was liberated quickly with relatively little expenditure of force—but had the invasion not taken place, the Germans would probably have had to retreat anyway or face constriction or attack from the north. There is certainly no evidence that they were desperate to hold onto the area following the Normandy invasion: there was no intention to counterattack landings in southern France or do anything other than retreat back towards the Vosges and hold the Alpine passes.

However, whatever detractors may say, there were two undeniably significant positives to come from the invasion. First, what it did for the French. Having been defeated in six weeks in 1940, spent four years under German rule, their government in exile having little voice militarily or politically, the success of what became French First Army provided a national fillip and much-needed pride. On top of this, the Maquis—the Resistance—provided considerable assistance to the invaders, and countered the hated *Milice* (Vichy France's paramilitary police). The men of the FFI (the *Forces Françaises de l'Intérior*)—a mixture of the Resistance and ex-servicemen—flocked to the banner as France was liberated. By the end of the war. France could point to 1.3 million men under arms—untrained, perhaps, but enthusiastic.

The second and more strategically important benefit of the invasion was the port of Marseille. Marseille is the same distance to Metz as Cherbourg is. With the latter's port so effectively destroyed (the main basins wouldn't

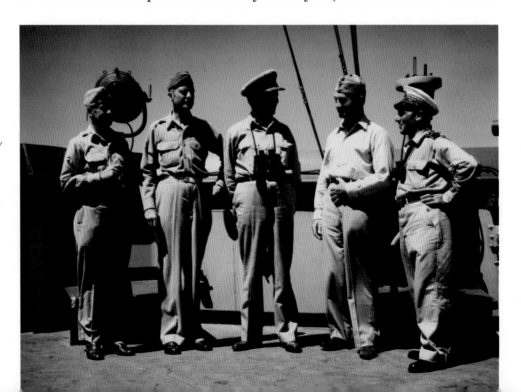

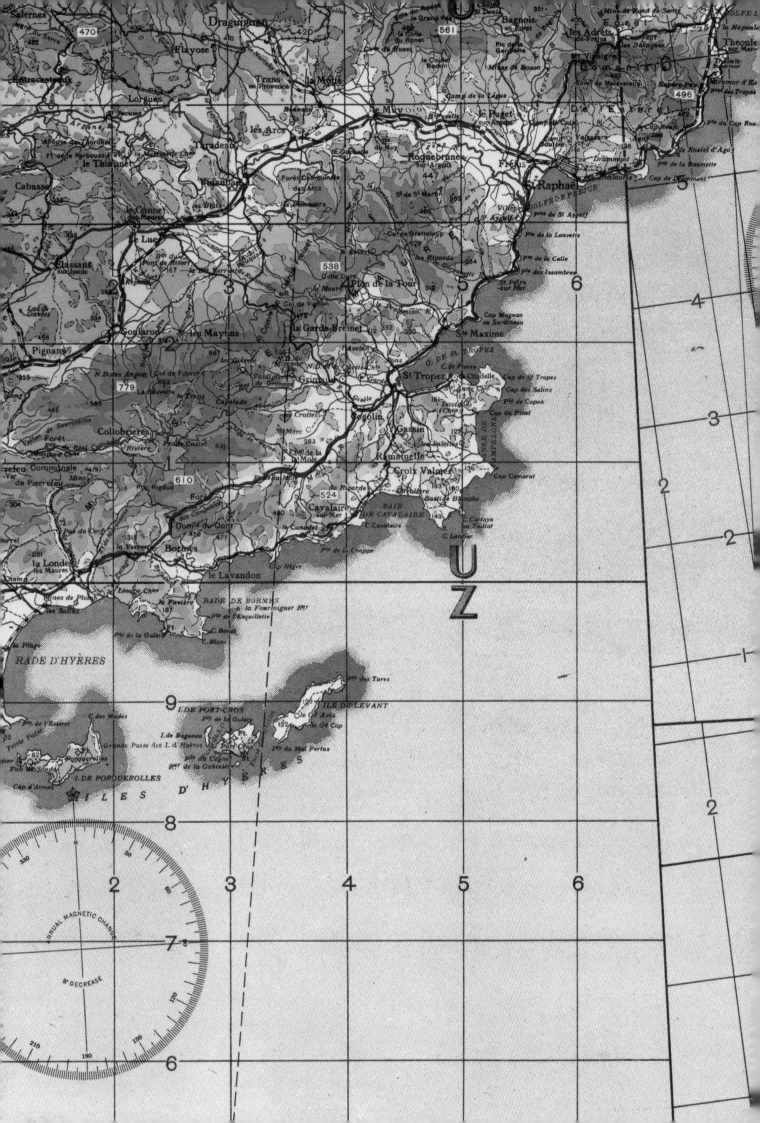

Above: *The VI Corps insignia — as can be seen on the shoulder of CG Lucien Truscott on p. 8.*

Below: *The US and British components of the landings. The French troops who would follow up are examined on page 89.*

be cleared until September 21), Brest and the Channel ports equally unavailable, Marseille became an important source of supplies in the US winter campaigns. The Germans had done their best to stop Marseille from being used, but the brilliant work of the US Army engineers and US Navy salvage teams saw the port up and running in late September.

So why the negatives? From the British point of view, taking forces away from Italy turned it into a sideshow. Churchill's "soft underbelly" had already proved to be anything but—and US Fifth Army commander Mark Clark had already made a serious strategic error in choosing the chimera of glory, taking Rome rather than cutting off the German Tenth Army's retreat. So when the US pulled three divisions and the French Expeditionary Force from Italy, it left Fifteenth Army Group commander General Sir Harold Alexander with fewer men than the German defenders, something even the arrival of the Brazilian Expeditionary Force could do little to improve.

The British had a longer term view: Churchill was thinking about postwar Europe. He viewed the likely Soviet domination of the Balkans and east Europe with disquiet and proposed landings in the Adriatic. The Germans were extremely worried about such an event—or a landing along the Ligurian Riviera. There is no doubt these concerns fixed forces in Italy that the Germans would have preferred to use elsewhere. More aggression in Italy may well have led to the collapse of Kesselring's position—he expected landings in Genoa—but the Western Allies fundamentally disagreed about this strategy. The Americans, with the war in Japan also in their minds, were more worried about British imperial ambitions than the Russians (something that would change shortly after the war with Britain bankrupt and the Iron Curtain coming down between east and west). In 1944, the Americans just wanted to finish off the Germans as quickly as possible so that they could concentrate on the Pacific and saw an invasion of the south of France and a broad front advance into Germany from the west as the easier way to go—and the ultimate short-term success of this approach makes it difficult to find fault with.

ORDER OF BATTLE OF US SEVENTH ARMY *(French components on p. 89)*
Commander: Lt-Gen. Alexander Patch

Army Troops
Included engineers, MPs, Medical, QM, Sigs, postal and port companies.

VI Corps
(CO: Maj-Gen Lucian K. Truscott)
HQ and HQ Coy
Combat Command Sudre (1DB): 1er Coy, 9RCA; engineer and ordnance troops
Field Artillery battalions: 36th, 59th, 69th, 93rd, 141st, 634th, 937th, 938th, 976th, 977th.
AAA Battalions: 68th, 72nd, 106th, 107th, 108th, 216th, 433rd, 441st, 443rd, 451st, 534th, 895th, and barrage balloon batteries
Armor: 191st, 753rd, and 756th Tank Battalion; 601st, 636th, and 645th TD Battalions
117th Cavalry Recon Squadron
Chemical: motorized battalions—2nd, 3rd, and 83rd
Engineer, Medical, MP, Ordnance, QM, Signals, and Naval liaison units

3rd Infantry Division
(CO: Maj-Gen John W. O'Daniel)
Divisional troops
7th, 15th, and 30th Infantry Regiments
Divisional artillery battalions: 9th, 10th, 39th, and 41st
Beach Group including Medical, Signals, MP (inc PoW Dept), Engr, Ordnance, QM

36th Infantry Division
(CO: Maj-Gen John E. Dahlquist)
Divisional troops
141st, 142nd, and 143rd Infantry Regiments
Divisional artillery battalions: 131st, 132nd, 133rd, and 155th
Beach Group including Medical, Signals, MP (inc PoW Dept), Engr, Ordnance, QM,

45th Infantry Division
(CO: Maj-Gen William W. Eagles)
Divisional troops
157th, 179th, and 180th Infantry Regiments
Divisional artillery battalions: 158th, 160th, 171st, and 189th
Beach Group including Medical, Signals, MP (inc PoW Dept), Engr, Ordnance, QM,

1st Airborne Task Force
(CO: Brig-Gen Robert T. Frederick)
US: 517th PIR (3 x battalions; 460th PFAB; 596th Airborne Engr Co)
509th PIB
1st Battalion, 551st PIR
463rd Airborne FA Battalion
550th PIB
602nd Glider FA Battalion
ATk Coy, 442nd Infantry Regiment
552nd ATk Coy (replaced 442nd Coy)
Various Sig, Med, Engr, Chem, Ord, MP
British: 2nd Ind Para Brigade Group (replaced after August 22 by US-Canadian 1st SSF)
4th Para Battalion
5th (Scottish) Para Battalion
6th (Royal Welch) Para Battalion
300th Airlanding ATk Battery, RA
64th Airlanding Battery, RA
2nd Para Squadron, RE
2nd Ind Para Brigade Group Coy, RSigs
1st Ind Glider Squadron (AAC)
Various Pathfinders, RASC, REME, RMP
30 French from 1RCP and Bataillon de Choc

The Allies

Before the opening of the Normandy front, the Mediterranean Theater was the only place that the Western Allies directly confronted the Germans on land, and the caliber of the commanders reflects this. Supreme commander from Operation Torch until he left for London to prepare for Normandy was Eisenhower, and his two main army commanders were the British victor of El Alamein, Bernard Montgomery who would become Eisenhower's land forces commander in Normandy, and the flamboyant American who commanded Seventh Army: George S. Patton, Jr.

Patton dominates the early history of the army. When the then major general's US I Armored Corps became Seventh Army on July 10, 1943, Patton was promoted lieutenant general and commanded the Seventh through the Sicilian campaign until early 1944—although after this its combat units were used in Italy under Fifth Army.

After Sicily, many of the key personnel in-theater began to move back to England to join Eisenhower preparing for the Normandy invasion. As Eisenhower put his existing team into place, so their places in the Mediterranean became free. Ike's successor was Field Marshal Sir Henry M. Wilson—better known as "Jumbo," who became Supreme Commander, Mediterranean Theater of Operations. Wilson's deputy was Lt Gen Jacob L. Devers, who had been moved from a potential role in Normandy when Eisenhower put Omar Bradley into place. Devers was also CG NATOUSA (North African Theater of Operations, US Army), and became CG of Sixth Army Group from August 1—he would take over control of US Seventh and FR First armies in France after the landing phase.

There were many other changes of personnel that affected the planning of Operation Dragoon: Ira Eaker was replaced by Jimmy Doolittle as commander of US Eighth Air Force and moved south to become commander-in-chief of the Mediterranean Air Force—replacing Arthur Tedder whom Eisenhower wanted in England. Patch became head of Seventh Army, then in reserve, on March 2, 1944. Initially, Mark Clark was destined to lead the invasion—it was his team that had been working on the invasion plans—but the problems at Anzio kept him in Italy and on February 15 Wilson agreed with Marshall and Devers that his place should be taken by Patch.

The other key member of the team that would execute Operation Dragoon was the commander of the naval side of the operation, Vice-Admiral Henry K. Hewitt, USN. The commander-in-chief of naval forces in the Mediterranean was Admiral Sir John Cunningham, RN. He created the Western Task Force and nominated Hewitt, the commander of US Eighth Fleet, to lead it.

Above: *US Sixth Army Group was activated on July 29, 1944 but Seventh Army controlled the landings and the advance up the Rhône valley. Once contact had been made with Third Army, Sixth Army Group took control of both US Seventh and French First armies. This is its insignia.*

Below, Left to Right: *Senior Allied commanders, L–R: Lt Gen Ira A. Eaker, MAAF; Maj Gen John A. Cannon, CG Twelfth Air Force; Lt Gen Jacob L. Devers, Deputy Supreme Commander of Allied Forces, Mediterranean Theater; Maj Gen Alexander M. Patch, CG Seventh Army; and Vice-Admiral H. Kent Hewitt, US Commander of the Fleet.*

GEN ALEXANDER McCARRELL "SANDY" PATCH
(November 23, 1889–November 21, 1945)

Underrated and unshowy, Sandy Patch was a professional soldier from an army family, who was born at Fort Huachuca, Arizona, in 1889. He went to West Point in 1909 and was commissioned into the 18th Infantry Regiment in Texas on June 12, 1913, seeing his first action in the Pancho Villa expedition to Mexico in 1916. In June 1917 he was promoted to captain in the 1st Infantry Division and went with the American Expeditionary Force to the Western Front, where he fought in the Second Battle of the Marne, the Battle of Saint-Mihel, and the Meuse-Argonne Offensive. After WWI he remained in the army and developed his talent as a trainer and organizer of fighting men. By November 1941 he was promoted to major general and sent to New Caledonia with a rudimentary improvised force to organize the defense of the 1,250-mile-long island.

Next he joined the Americal Division and took part in the Guadalcanal Campaign in December 1942, before in January 1943 he took command of XIV Corps and control over the whole offensive, going on to defeat and expel the Japanese Forces by February 1943—the first US victory of the war. In March 1944 he took command of the Seventh Army, composed of various veteran French and American units transferred from Africa and the Italian campaign, including Maj Gen Lucian Truscott's US VI Corps and General Alphonse Juin's French Expeditionary Corps as well as American, French, and British airborne units.

Turning soldiers from three continents into a cohesive fighting unit, Patch's Seventh Army invaded southern France in Operation Dragoon, and he was promoted to lieutenant general after the successful landings. He handled the predominantly joint American and French forces with delicacy and tact, allowing the French to spearhead the attack after the landings and liberate Toulon and Marseille. He then led the Seventh on a fast offensive up the Rhone valley, linking up with Patton's Third Army around Dijon on September 9, 1944, before the difficult but ultimately successful winter campaign in the Vosges Mountains—with some of Europe's worst conditions and toughest terrain in which to conduct operations.

Having had a lot of his men and resources siphoned off to other theaters and now with a single corps under his command, Patch continued to push forward. He eventually received nine incompletely trained infantry regiments which he mixed in with his veterans. The Seventh then stopped the Germans final counteroffensive (Operation Nordwind), crossed over the Rhine and broke through the Siegfried Line into southern Germany. Tragically his only son, Capt Alexander M. Patch III, was killed in action on October 22 while serving as an infantry company commander in the 315th Infantry Regiment of the 79th Infantry Division—part of Patch's army. Hating the limelight and avoiding publicity, Patch stayed focused on the job in hand and the welfare of his troops. He remained the Seventh's commander until the end of hostilities and all who fought for him and wrote about it afterwards are full of admiration and affection.

In August 1945 he returned to the United States to take command of the Fourth Army, but he was completely worn out. Having endured pneumonia in New Caledonia and tropical dysentery and malaria on Guadalcanal, he now succumbed to pneumonia once again and died on November 21, 1945, two days short of his 56th birthday. He was posthumously promoted to General and buried at West Point Cemetery in the grounds of the USMA.

Above: *Patch was a major-general commanding forces in New Caledonia when this photograph was taken.* Library of Congress

Below Left: *Seventh Army insignia—Seven Steps to Hell.*

Below: *Promoted lieutenant general three days after the Dragoon landings, Patch proved an able leader and commanded Seventh Army to the end of the war.* Pennsylvania State Archives

Air Support

Lt Gen Ira C. Eaker's Mediterranean Allied Air Forces was split into three commands: MATAF—Tactical—was commanded by the CG of US Twelfth Air Force, Maj Gen John K. Cannon; MACAF—Coastal—by AVM Sir Hugh P. Lloyd, RAF; and MASAF—Strategic—by CG US Fifteenth Air Force, Maj Gen Nathan F. Twining. As in Normandy, air support was crucial to the operation: first, bombers were used to isolate the battlefield, ensuring that reinforcements would struggle to use rail transport or cross road or rail bridges over the major rivers; interdiction of enemy troop movements and cutting lines of communication was helped by almost complete air superiority. Second, the coastal and island batteries and troop positions were bombarded before the invasion to reduce their combat effectiveness. Third, the early morning of D-Day saw the dropping of paratroopers to help take the high ground and open routes off the beaches. Finally, air operations continued to maintain air superiority over the area of the landings and further afield.

Above: *The building of airstrips was an imperative to extend close-support and fighter cover. It also allowed casualty evacuation and supply. (See map on p. 111.)*

Below: *Bombing operations helped suppress German batteries and isolate the battlefield.*

Above and Right: *The Anthéor viaduct still serves the coastal railway that meanders between Saint-Raphaël and Cannes, part of the line from Marseille to Nice completed in 1864. This was on the eastern edge of the landings and was brought down by Allied bombing to ensure that the landings area was isolated. A plaque on the viaduct remembers 36th Infantry Division's 1/141st Regiment's landings (***Inset***).*

Allied air support of the Riviera landings was substantial. As well as the bombing campaign before the landings, it was there to help as necessary: bombers were used on Camel Red when the landings struck difficulties. During the battle of Toulon, the hold out Saint-Mandrier-sur-Mer peninsula with its heavy artillery batteries, was turned into a moonscape it was so heavily bombed. The problems with air support came later. First, the provision of forward landing strips took longer than expected. Postwar VI Corps commander Lucien Truscott was scathing about this, blaming the problems of the landings at Camel Red but as Clarke and Smith say, his remarks are difficult to support. Nevertheless, XII TAC had serious range problems caused by the speed of the advance, which rendered Corsica—nicknamed XII TAC's aircraft carrier because of the number of airbases on it—out of range. The needs of the Italian campaign also intruded, particularly in September. Without close-air support, XII TAC was able to wreak havoc on the Nineteenth Army columns north of Montélimar but proved unable to provide timely interventions, this "convincingly demonstrated that interdiction operations cannot substitute for true close-air support, which might have supplied the firepower needed by ground units when other support assets were lacking."

Sur cette plage d'Anthéor, objectif dangereux du secteur Est du débarquement de Provence, le 1er Bataillon du 141ème Régiment de la 36ème Division d'Infanterie de l'U.S. Army prit pied le 15 Août 1944. Son héroïsme, sa bravoure et son esprit de corps furent récompensés par une *Presidential Unit Citation* décernée par le Général Dwight D. Eisenhower.

Cette plaque a été posée par la Mairie de Saint-Raphaël

The Germans

After the November 1942 Allied landings in North Africa the Germans took control of Vichy France and began an attempt to fortify its 300 miles of Mediterranean coastline. This was divided into seven different sectors from A to G, with special defensive zones around the critical naval port of Toulon and at Marseille, where the Organization Todt U-boat pens were built in 1943. Existing French bunkers and gun emplacements were taken over and enhanced—French battleship guns were already in place guarding Toulon and the Vichy government had built over 70 heavy gun emplacements and mounted turrets—but new structures were built in other vulnerable locations, flanked by extensive barbed wire, tank traps, minefields, beach obstacles, and over 600 pillboxes.

The defeat of Axis forces in North Africa and the invasion of Sicily and Italy in 1943 gave the work a new urgency and Rommel's inspection and advice did much to improve things. Many French, Italian, and other captured guns were used—their turrets taken from warships and tanks and incorporated into stand-alone and bunker systems. The tank turrets were mainly French or German Panzer IIs. Built later than the Atlantic Wall, the Südwall had fewer fortifications, with many of them still uncompleted when Operation Dragoon began, but because of these plundered weapons it had a high number of coastal artillery pieces — although of a bewildering variety. The Kriegsmarine used naval guns that

Above: *Another bridge collapses after attack by B-25 medium bombers. German movement into Provence was hampered by these operations, and while repairing the damage would require considerable hard work, the immediate benefits were obvious.*

Below: *Army Group G had been denuded as troops were sent to help stem the tide in Normandy. Blaskowitz and Wiese knew where the hammer was going to fall but were unable to concentrate sufficient force to stop the bridgehead expanding. Unlike Normandy, where the defenders were able to reinforce the defenses and use their armor and the terrain to hold the Allies in place for two months, in the south there was little they could do other than retreat.*

ORDER OF BATTLE OF ARMY GROUP G IN SOUTHERN FRANCE
Commander: Generaloberst Johannes Blaskowitz

ARMY GROUP G HQ (Toulouse)

NINETEENTH ARMY (Avignon)
(CO: General der Infanterie Friedrich Wiese)

Army Reserve
11. Panzer-Division (Generalmajor Wend von Wietersheim) ordered east towards Avignon
157. Reserve Division (Generalleutnant Karl Pflaum) redesignated 157. Gebirgs-Division in September 1944
158. Reserve Division (Generalleutnant Ernst Häckel) planned to reform 16. Infantry Division, but the latter was reformed as it was instead reformed as 16. Volksgrenadier-Division

LXXXV Army Corps (Marseille)
(CO: Gen der Infanterie Baptist Kniess)
338. Infantry Division (Generalleutnant René l'Homme de Coubière) less one regiment sent north; other elements due to follow
244. Infantry Division (Generalleutnant Hans Schaefer)

LXII Army Corps (Draguignan)
(CO: Gen der Infanterie Ferdinand Neuling)
242. Infantry Division (Generalleutnant Johannes Baessler)
148. Reserve Infantry Division (Generalmajor Otto Fretter-Pico)

IV Luftwaffe Field Corps (Montpellier)
(CO: Generalleutnant Erich Pietersen)
189. Infantry Division (Generalleutnant Richard von Schwerin), Grenadier Regiment 18 of which was in reserve near Carcassonne Gap
198. Infantry Division (Generalmajor Alfred Kuhnert) which had been ordered east to act as LXXXV Corps reserve
716. Infantry Division (Generalmajor Otto Schiel) refitting after having been destroyed defending against the Normandy invasion

There were also a number of liaison staffs (Verbindungsssstab; pl: -stäbe) under Heeresgebiet Südfrankreich

were bolted to the foundations on pedestal mounts, operating 37 batteries of mainly French and German guns in two separate commands. The Heer used an even more diverse selection of some 270 German, French, Russian, Italian, Czech, and other field guns, that could usually be removed from their concrete bunkers and resited using a back door built into the casemate. The most common French gun was the 138mm KM1910(f) but there were a number of German naval guns from destroyers or U-Boot deck guns. There was also an army railroad artillery unit of four German (2 x 380mm and 2 x 280mm) and three French 274mm guns (see p.132). For more on the armament of the Südwall see Steven Zaloga's excellent title in the Osprey "Fortress" series.)

Above: *11. Panzer Division PzKpfw IVs motor east through Toulouse. It had been covering the southwest of France when ordered east and was in no position to affect the fighting around the Riviera. Its progress was hampered by the Allied interdiction of the landing areas—particularly the destruction of the bridges over the Rhône—and the German Army's usual weakness: lack of motorized transport. The closest the division got to the Riviera was Aix-en-Provence.*

Left: *Hitler's "defend to the last man" policy was never considered viable by the defenders of southern France. With little or no assistance from the Italian front, the constant Maquis assassinations, ambushes and sabotage, weakened and substandard defensive formations, and faced by the overwhelming might of the Allies, it's unsurprising the Germans preferred a fighting retreat. In fact, other than various ports, Hitler rescinded his order on August 16 and the retreat was approved. The forces shown here were supplemented by both naval and army coastal batteries.*

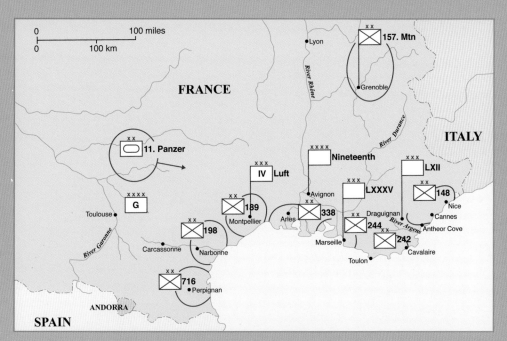

17

With both Kriegsmarine and Heer having coastal batteries and separate command structures, it is unsurprising that it proved ineffective. Had Vizeadmiral Ernst Scheulen—a coastal artillery specialist—been in charge earlier, things might have been different, but he didn't take over the position until August 17 by which time the invasion was a fait accompli. Added to this was the lack of German warships to harass the Allied warships that were able, pretty much without contest, to support the invasion and then the advance along the coast.

The labyrinthine German coastal artillery command structure reflected the problems seen in its higher command processes, with overlapping areas of responsibility, direct input from the wild card Hitler, little integration of Heer and Kriegsmarine with the Luftwaffe, and a mixture of defensive philosophies.

Army Group G defended southern France from invasion. Commanded by Oberstgeneral Johannes Blaskowitz since May 1944, it had seen much of its strength reduced after the Normandy invasion. It had lost in June and July 17. SS-Panzergrenadier Division, LXXXVI and LVIII Panzer Corps HQs, two Panzer divisions (2. SS *Das Reich* and 9.), five infantry divisions, four artillery battalions, two assault gun battalions, four assault gun training battalions, and five infantry training battalions. In August there were more losses: the First Army (which controlled the west Atlantic coastline), LXVI, and LXXX Corps HQs; a regimental combat team from 338. Infantry Division (the rest of the division was preparing to move north), two artillery

battalions, an infantry replacement battalion, a tank battalion from 11. Panzer, and various AAA and ATk units.

The movement wasn't all one way, but the troops who replaced those moving north weren't of high standard. LXIV Corps HQ replaced First Army on the Atlantic coast with 716. Infantry—decimated on the Normandy coast; and 189. Infantry moved to near Montpellier to take over from 338. Infantry; two antitank and a heavy artillery battalion.

The divisions that opposed Operation Dragoon had been further weakened with their best men taken north and *Osttruppen*—Russian and other soldiers from the Eastern Front who had "volunteered" to serve with the Germans, either through coercion or preferring that to becoming PoWs.

There was one other possible location of assistance for Nineteenth Army when the invasion took place: Italy. However, with German eyes elsewhere—Kesselring was expecting an attack on either the Ligurian or Adriatic coasts—there was never any likelihood of support, and the Allies knew this. The forces sent to clear the Riviera advanced to the Italian border and remained there, keeping a wary eye on the Alpine passes for any threat. None accrued.

The result was that the Allies were able to land, roll up the coast and then the Rhône valley with little significant opposition. The fixed—*bodenständig*—divisions were lost; the mobile units retreated and some were able to reach the safety of the Vosges where they were able to bog down the Sixth Army Group in bitter fighting. However, German casualties amounted to well over 150,000—including Army Group G's losses of 7,000 killed and over 100,000 captured.

Opposite, Above: *General der Infanterie Friedrich Wiese (1892–1975) commanded German Nineteenth Army June–December 15, 1944. An experienced officer who had been awarded the Ritterkreuz in April 1942 and the Oak Leaves in January 1944, he had worked his way up from command of an infantry battalion in Infantry Regiment 116 before commanding Regiment 39, next 26. Infantry Division then XXXV Armeekorps on the Eastern Front from August 1943. On taking over Nineteenth Army, Blaskowitz, commanding Army Group G, told him to beef up the Südwall. He did, but to no avail. His fighting retreat up the Rhône valley may have saved the bulk of his army, but in December he was relieved of his command.*

Left: *German prisoners of war in St. Tropez, France on August 18.*

Below: *Marine-Flak-Abteilung 819 at La Renardière had four SKC32 105mm Flak guns in cupolas on FL316 bunkers. In the background, the fire direction station. The Saint Mandrier peninsula overlooked Toulon, part of the extensive defenses of France's largest port.*

11. Panzer Division

Gespensterdivision—the Ghost Division

Named after its spectral unit insignia, 11. Panzer Division was formed in August 1940 in the German province of Silesia. At its core were Panzer Regiment 15, taken from 5. Panzer Division, and elements of three infantry divisions. Over the course of the war it would be decimated or worse a number of times, yet each time be rebuilt from a nucleus of capable and experienced unit commanders and NCOs, and an outstanding commander from August 10, 1943, in Generalmajor Wend von Wietersheim.

Its first combat was in the April 1941 invasion of Yugoslavia. It was then sent to the Eastern Front as part of First Panzer Army of Army Group South, where it participated in the battles around Kiev and, from October 1941, in the battle of Moscow. After the failure to capture the city and having suffered heavy losses, 11. Panzer was posted to the central section of the eastern front in the Gshatsk area where it was rebuilt. In June 1942, it was moved to the southern sector to be part of the 1942 German summer offensive that continued Operation Barbarossa. Initial successes at Voronezh and Stalingrad were thwarted in the end by tenacious Russian resistance and overstretched supply lines which left the German forces vulnerable to counterattacks.

11. Panzer avoided entrapment in Stalingrad but suffered heavy losses that winter. It was part of the failed attempt to relieve Sixth Army and then helped in the defense of Rostov, enabling German troops to escape from the Caucasus. Next, in July 1943 it took part in the battle of Kursk and the subsequent fighting retreat following its failure.

In February 1944 it was caught in

xx
☐ **11. Panzer**
January 1945

September–December
Counterattacks add to Patton's fuel problems and curtail Third Army's drive to the Westwall.

September 3
11. Panzer counterattack defeats elements of French I Corps near Montbéliard.

September 3
11. Panzer-Aufklärungs-Bataillon mauls US 117th Cavalry Recon Sqn near Montreval.

August 31
Battle of Meximieux
with US 45th Inf Div

August 21
Kampfgruppen of 11. Panzer attack US 36th Inf Div and TF Butler thus enabling Nineteenth Army's continued retreat.

xx
☐ **11. Panzer**
August 13

BELGIUM
Bitburg
LUXEMBOURG
GERMANY
Verdun
Metz
Morhange
Arracourt
Nancy
Saverne
Chaumont
Épinal
FRANCE
Belfort
Montbéliard
Dijon
Besançon
SWITZERLAND
Chalon-sur-Saône
Geneva
Montreval
Bourg-en-Bresse
Meximieux
Lyon
ITALY
Grenoble
Montélimar
Avignon
Aix-en-Provence
Nîmes
Saint-Tropez
Beziers
Marseille
Carcassonne
Toulon
Narbonne
SPAIN
ANDORRA

| 0 | | 100 miles |
| 0 | | 100 km |

the Korsun-Cherkassy Pocket and almost completely destroyed in the breakout. It was then withdrawn and sent to Bordeaux in southern France, where it was once again rebuilt and reassigned to the Nineteenth Army around Toulouse.

Following the June 1944 Normandy Landings, 11. Panzer was moved westward to defend the Bordeaux area, so when the Allies invaded southern France in August 1944 it was still out of position and could not properly oppose the initial bridgehead. (It was the only mobile strike force for all of Army Group G south of the Loire.) It then fought a steady withdrawal up the Rhône corridor to Besançon.

Several times the more mobile US Seventh Army attempted to cut off Nineteenth Army, but was thwarted by the 11. Panzer, using its battle experience and dwindling resources to good effect, at Montélimar, Meximieux, and Montrevel. Using the Kampfgruppe concept of mixed battle groups—a mixture of Panzer and Panzergrenadier units that were used to operating independently—it gained a reputation against those it fought as an able but honorable opponent who looked after captured wounded. Retreating into Alsace, it defended the Belfort Gap and took part in the battle of Arracourt before returning to the Saar in Germany, to be beefed up once again.

In December 1944 11. Panzer then participated in the battle of the Bulge and following that operation's failure once again withdrew, fighting in Saarland, Moselle, and Remagen. Its final combat came defending the Ruhr, where the German Army Group B was encircled and destroyed by US and British forces, though 11. Panzer managed to avoid capture. Drifting eastward it was finally cornered just inside the western border of Czechoslovakia and technically within the Soviet sphere of control. Disobeying a command to return to Berlin and in order to avoid surrendering to the Soviets, Generalmajor von Wietersheim surrendered to the Americans, and with the Ghost Division's good reputation amongst US generals Patton and Bradley (and their natural antipathy to the Soviets) it was allowed to recross the border and surrender intact to the US 90th Infantry Division.

Above: *Wend von Wietersheim (1900–75) started his military career as a cavalry officer in WWI, during which he was awarded the Iron Cross (2nd class). He would add a clasp to the Iron Cross, an Iron Cross (1st class), and the Knight's Cross 1939–1942, going on to gain the oak leaves while commander of PzGr Regiment 113 in 1943 and swords in 1944 while a Generalmajor commanding 11. Panzer.*

Below Left: *11. Panzer Division PzKpfw IV in Yugoslavia in 1941—note the divisional symbol next to the Balkankreuz beneath the turret. By 1944 the division was equipped with only one company of PzKpfw IVs armed with the longer-barreled L/48 and a battalion of PzKpfw V Panthers. It also had an antitank battalion, four infantry battalions and an artillery regiment as well as engineers and other divisional troops. The division did not see as much action on the retreat as might have been expected, and crossed the Drôme with at least 75 percent of its manpower and most of its tanks intact.* Bundesarchiv/Wikimedia

General Blaskowitz commanded German Army Group G, whose infantry divisions were of mixed abilities. The coast between Spain and Italy was not as well defended as Normandy, and there were few effective reserves. What there were—elements of LXII Corps—were commanded by three men who had been relieved of duties in Russia for health reasons. On top of this, the Luftwaffe was practically nonexistent, and the Allies had good air coverage—better once advance airstrips had been built. Blaskowitz conducted a fighting retreat up the Rhône valley, and is regarded as one of the best German generals, whom Hitler ended up using in spite of his apparent grudge against him.

OBERSTGENERAL JOHANNES BLASKOWITZ
(July 10, 1883–February 5, 1948)

Johannes Albrecht Blaskowitz was born on July 10, 1883, in Peterswalde, East Prussia (now Cierznie in northern Poland). In 1894 he attended the local cadet college in Köslin, then later the prestigious Berlin Lichterfelde Military Academy and in March 1901 joined an East Prussian Army regiment in Osterode as a non-commissioned officer. By January 1910 he was a second lieutenant and a captain by February 1914.

During WWI he served on both fronts as an infantry company commander, being wounded and winning the Iron Cross for bravery. His war record ensured his survival as an army officer in the Weimar Republic during the interwar years, working his way up the officer ranks through ability and merit, by 1933 he was a lieutenant general. Being an honorable and traditional professional Prussian officer, Blaskowitz believed politics to be outside the army's remit and thus was indifferent to the Nazi Party's rise to power. In 1936 he was promoted to general and having proven his competency during the annexation of Austria and occupation of Czechoslovakia, in September 1939 he was given command of the German Eighth Army during the invasion of Poland. His success in that campaign won him the Knight's Cross, promotion to Oberstgeneral and the appointment to Commander-in-Chief East.

It was at this time that Blaskowitz became aware of systematic atrocities being committed against Polish civilians by the Waffen-SS and other groups within the Nazi administration. Outraged and disgusted, he collected evidence and officially complained—repeatedly. When his complaints reached Hitler in May 1940 he was promptly relieved of his command and relegated, first to a minor military governor's position in Northern France, then to command First Army on the Spanish border.

There he remained sidelined until the very different situation of May 1944, when Generalfeldmarschall Gerd von Rundstedt gave him command of Army Group G, tasked with the defense of Southern France. After the Allied invasion of Normandy in June 1944 Army Group G had been reduced in size and capability as some of its best elements were sent north to bolster the German defense, thus when the Allied invasion of southern France began it was stretched too thinly to put up much of a fight.

With the arrival of 11. Panzer Division, Blaskowitz was able to conduct a clever fighting withdrawal up the Rhone valley and over the Vosges Mountains for which he was awarded Oak Leaves to his Knight's Cross. Then on December 31, 1944, he took part in the final German offensive on the Western Front, Operation Nordwind, launched in conjunction with the Ardennes Offensive. Both operations forced by an increasingly deranged Führer were costly failures and used up the last German reserves in the West. Army Group G under Blaskowitz fought well, for which he earned Swords to his Knight's Cross, and was next sent to the Netherlands to take command of Army Group H.

Fighting against British and Canadian forces he conducted another orderly fighting withdrawal that proved costly for the Allies. He ignored Hitler's orders for the total destruction of Dutch infrastructure and industry and cooperated with the Allies concerning the food supplies for the starving civilians during the terrible winter of 1944–1945. On May 7 he surrendered all German forces in the Netherlands. Arrested and imprisoned at the war's end, in 1948 he was charged with war crimes at the Nuremberg High Command Trial, but given his documented exception to Nazi methods was expected to be acquitted. However, before the trial got underway he died under mysterious circumstances, either by committing suicide leaping from a balcony, or being thrown off by SS prisoners who didn't trust him to keep silent.

Left: *US Navy sailor examines a German 20mm Panzer II tank turret "pillbox," near one of the invasion beaches, August 18. The Südwall defenses incorporated a number of these and other similar bunkers including APX R (see pp. 2–3) and others from French tanks, as well as those from the PzKpfw 38(t).*

Below Left: *As in Normandy, the Südwall was undergoing continuous upgrading and work was going on when the invasion took place. These partially completed beach obstacles are on Cavalaire Beach. Note, the white tape marks suspected minefields.*

Below: *Trenches on Red Beach in Alpha Sector. In the sea, soldiers on a stranded truck wait to unload its contents.*

Above: *The face of battle—these are men of 157th Infantry Regiment, 45th Division who had spent a week surrounded in hostile territory in December 1944. The early days of the campaign saw light opposition, decent weather, and speedy success. September saw a more tenacious defense and, as the weather worsened in fall and winter, casualties mounted. In one area, however, Seventh Army was better equipped than other US forces: uniform and footwear. Supplied through the Mediterranean theater, there was ample provision both of the new M1943 jacket—superior when used with wool underwear and jumpers than the heavy greatcoat—and of shoepacs. These weren't perfect but when allied to sensible advice about caring for feet, they were better than other boots. Trenchfoot and cold weather injuries were a serious problem in the European theater in 1944: in Seventh Army the main issue was that those who had suffered in the Italian cold in 1943 were more likely to suffer again. The official medical history of the war identified that "Fifty percent of the cases in the Seventh US Army were recurrences in men who had suffered from cold injury in Italy the previous year."*

Below: *Until the end of September the weather in southern France had been typical—for the most part dry, warm, and clement. All that changed as the fall arrived. "It proved to be the wettest winter, as well as the coldest, that Europe had experienced in 30 years. The heavy rains which began early in October continued throughout the month. On the Third US Army front, it rained 28 of the 31 days.*

"The offensive was conducted in large part over wet and flooded terrain and required the crossing of major rivers. The Moselle and other rivers were high because of the immoderate rains. By November, flood conditions had become general in all army areas. Fields and roads were water soaked, and irrigation ditches and small streams as well as rivers were all overflowing. The weather was always cold, and cold injuries, in the form of trench-foot, occurred in great numbers." In his book, A Soldier's Story, Gen. Omar N. Bradley, Commanding General, 12th Army Group, presents the military interpretation of these losses. By the end of January 1945, he wrote, "cold injury had seriously crippled the United States fighting strength in Europe."

The Terrain and the Weather

The geography of southern France, known as the Midi, is bordered by the Pyrenees and Spain to the west and by the Alps and Italy to the east and contains the regions of Aquitaine, Languedoc, and Provence. To the north, the southern end of the Massif Central extends into Languedoc, pierced by the Rhône flowing down to its delta and the Mediterranean. The southern coast of France and its hinterland is conveniently divided into two sections by the Rhone, its delta beginning at Avignon and stretching to Montpellier in the west and Aix-en-Provence in the east. All traffic along the coast must pass this delta to gain access to the hinterland or to the other length of coastline.

The Mediterranean climate predominates in the south and southeast, stretching inland from the coast to the lower Rhône valley. Winters are mild and humid, with only short periods of frost, and the summers are hot and dry. However, as one travels farther north, so the rain and snow fall levels grow.

The French Riviera, where the Dragoon landings took place, is a thin coastal strip from around Cassis (east of Marseille) in the west to the Italian border in the east. The Allied planners discounted a direct assault on the major ports of Toulon and Marseille with their formidable seaward fortifications and chose instead the Saint-Tropez area some 30 miles to the east. The beachhead included 50 miles of coastline to an inland depth of 20 miles, encompassing the Maures and Esterel hill masses. This area had several excellent landing sites with good access into the interior.

Possession of this terrain allowed Allied forces to travel along the coastal roads northeast towards Cannes and west to Toulon, and move up the Argens River valley—an east–west corridor that begins just north of the Massif des Maures. In the event the landing zone was relatively poorly defended and soon expanded. A large airborne force dropped inland to secure the high ground behind the beaches during the night of August 14–15 and commando teams liberated several islands along the coast. Possession of the Le Muy area protected the initial landings and provided an entrance into the Argens valley corridor.

Below: *Between December 19, 1944, and January 31, 1945, the average maximum temperature at the front in Europe was 33.5°F, and the average minimum temperature 22.6°F. It is in conditions like these that the success or otherwise of military logistics comes into play. Have the soldiers been provided with adequate cold weather equipment—particularly footgear? Do they and their medical teams know enough about the hazards of wet and cold weather on feet? As a whole, 1944 was a learning curve for the military and the suffering at the front was made worse for a number of reasons, but in the end it was just poor planning. There are two main extenuating circumstances: first, in August everyone thought the war would be over by Xmas and didn't make suitable provision for cold weather gear. They gambled that they wouldn't need it in theater and when it became obvious that they did, getting sufficient quantities to Europe and then distributed to the troops proved impossible until late January 1945. Second, the sheer increase in numbers of troops was hard to predict: on May 31, 1942, there were 34,350 US Army troops in Europe; a year later when the war ended that figure had risen to over three million.*

The Resistance

The Resistance in France during World War II was a composite of different groups and networks from all political persuasions and social backgrounds who fought against the German occupation and the collaborators of the Vichy government through whom they ruled. Due to so many French men being held in prison camps or sent as slave workers to Germany, there was also a high proportion of women within their ranks. They began divided, as small self-contained cells to avoid betrayal, more often than not unarmed, producing underground newspapers and setting up escape networks for Allied airmen, spies, and political refugees. The Free French government in London formed their own Bureau of Intelligence and Operations—BCRA (*Bureau central de Renseignements et d'Action*) in an attempt to coordinate the many groups. The British for their part formed the Special Operations Executive (SOE) in 1941 to train and equip some of their own cells. At first, these groups were often very amateurish. The Germans didn't acknowledge them as bona fide soldiers but treated them instead as terrorists, encouraging betrayal and appealing to prejudice through bribery and corruption. When caught they were tortured, turned, or murdered, along with their friends, families, and neighbors as the Nazis conducted increasingly vicious reprisals against the general population.

After the June 1941 German invasion of Russia, the well-organized communist Francs-Tireurs et Partisans (FTP) groups joined the side of the Resistance in earnest. By 1942 de Gaulle, always keen on trying to control the many differing groups, established contact with them. That year saw an intensification of proceedings with the first French Jews sent to Auschwitz. Still more French men disappeared to Germany and there was an influx of volunteers escaping these German purges.

In December a new resistance group, the Army Resistance Organization (Organisation de Résistance de l'Armée, ORA), was founded, receiving support from the US. In January 1943, a key Resistance leader, Jean

Below: *Supplied by airdrops and the SOE—the British Special Operations Executive—the French Resistance played a significant role in the invasion. Known as Maquisards, forming Maquis units, the resistance hardened after the STO (Service du travail obligatoire) was set up in February 1943. This compulsory labor service meant that unemployed men were sent to Germany to work (over 600,000 French workers went to Germany). One step up from slave laborers, many preferred to stay hidden in France and joined the Resistance—and the numbers swelled as the Allied armies breached the Atlantic Wall.*

Above: *In France, as in every country subjugated by the Germans, there were collaborators. Some, with similar political views, were willing accomplices—many were simply forced to collaborate to survive. The Holocaust saw 75,000 Jews—of the 340,000 in France—deported: 72,500 died. The French Vichy regime was complicit in these deportations. After the Allies arrived in France, the punishments for the collaborators began. At one end there was the shaving of the heads of women who had consorted with the enemy; at the other, important government figures such as Pétain and Laval or the novelist Louis-Ferdinand Céline, who wrote anti-Semitic pamphlets. Some 10,000 French men and women died during and just after the liberation as summary justice—and score settling— was carried out. This photograph was taken in Apt on August 26.*

Right: *There are many photographs of Resistance members armed with German weapons they had stripped from their opponents. This Marquisard in Brignoles on August 19 has acquired an MG34 and drum magazine, a couple of bayonets, a Kar98 and magazine pouch, as well as a stick grenade and helmet.*

Top: *Armed with an American .30-cal. and Sten guns, this FFI team is in Apt on August 22.*

Above: *They may not have been in uniform—or even fully clothed—but the Maquisards proved a thorn in the side of the German garrisons.*

Opposite, Above: *The remains of a German glider at Vassieux.*

Opposite, Below: *The memorial and graveyard at Vassieux.*

Moulin, having conferred with de Gaulle in London, persuaded the three main resistance groups in the south of France —the FTP, Liberation and Combat—to unite as the United Resistance Movement (*Mouvements Unis de Résistance*, MUR), whose armed wing was the Secret Army (*Armée Secrète*, AS). By this time the name *Maquis* (wild scrub), formerly that of rural guerilla bands of the south, was being used as a collective word for the Resistance, which was becoming increasingly organized. That same month the Germans created the *Milice*, manned by brutal French fascists and gangsters, to hunt down and destroy the Maquis by any means necessary.

As assassinations and acts of sabotage and ambush became more frequent, so large-scale operations and reprisals against innocent civilians grew, carried out by the Wehrmacht, the SS or the Gestapo themselves, as well as the Milice. Moulin was betrayed and murdered in July 1943, but immediately replaced. In February 1944, all the Resistance groups agreed to accept the authority of the Free French government based in Algiers but controlled from London by de Gaulle, and they were formerly renamed the FFI (*Forces Françaises de l'Intérieur*, or Forces of the Interior). The FFI played an important part in and after the Allied landings in Europe, supplying information, destroying infrastructure critical to the German supply system, and launching synchronized attacks in their rear.

As the Allies progressed, the FFI numbers swelled to over 400,000 by October 1944 and a nervous de Gaulle made sure they were increasingly incorporated into the Free French military, so that by the end of the war France had an army of some 1.2 million men.

Vassieux-en-Vercors

The Vercors Massif is a dramatic range of mountains and plateaux in the French Préalpes that snakes across the regions of Isère and Drôme. Although not excessively high (2,341m/7,680ft) it is difficult to access, and so during WWII it became a natural redoubt for the French Resistance. Soon after the fall of France the town of Vassieux-en-Vercors became one of the main centers of the local Maquis and gradually a plan named "Montagnard" was evolved with the Free French government in exile, to deliver and stockpile arms in preparation for the seizure of the massif after the forthcoming Allied invasion. Following the implementation of the February 1943 STO requiring all able-bodied Frenchmen to work in Germany, many more volunteers flocked to Vercors, including some communist FTP, who advocated a confrontation with the Germans to inflame public opinion and stimulate a general uprising rather than wait to join the Allied advance. Although it was supposed to be a hidden base, in November 1943 Vercors received its first parachute drop of weapons and equipment. This increased activity prompted a German response with an attack in January 1944 and again on April 16–24 when a vicious counter-insurgency operation was carried out by the Milice.

Following the D-Day landings, hundreds more volunteers converged on Vercors and the Maquis, at the behest of the FFI, activated Plan Montagnard, securing the Vercors Massif and beginning to build a landing strip outside Vassieux. By July 3 they numbered some 4,000 and the Free Republic of Vercors was passionately proclaimed. Between June 25 and July 12 the Allies then dropped over a thousand containers of arms, ammunition, equipment, and supplies onto the plateau, though no heavy weapons were landed. In retaliation the Germans repeatedly bombed Vassieux, destroying half the town. Then on July 18, Operation Bettina, under the command of Generalleutnant Karl Pflaum, was launched. With armor, artillery, and air support over 10,000 men, including elements of the 157. Reserve (Gebirgs) Division, along with mobile units of the 9. Panzer Division, supported by 500 troops from the Milice, began encircling then attacking the plateau. On July 21 two Ostlegion (Russian, Ukrainian, and Caucasian) companies making up Fallschirm-Bataillon Jungwirth then airlanded in gliders at Vassieux.

Encircled and trapped, in the ensuing fierce combat and its grisly post-battle hunt and torture almost 1,000 Maquisards and civilians perished. In the intensity of the battle the Germans lost some 350 men. This particularly vicious suppression of the Vercors insurrection did succeed in inflaming public anger and increasing resistance, but it also proved that without heavy weapons the Maquis were neither well enough equipped to take on the German Army, nor well enough organized. "Montagnard" had been launched too early and was doomed—flawed by being compromised in a power struggle between the FFI in Algiers and de Gaulle in London, besides being before Operation Dragoon and, therefore, before the Maquisards could link up with any other Allied ground forces. Avoiding any further attempt at other large-scale tactical operations, the Maquis returned to a guerilla war of sabotage, assassination, and ambush until their attacks could be coordinated with arrival of the Allies.

1 PLANS AND PREPARATIONS

This is what the arsenal of democracy could provide: a seemingly limitless stockpile of motorized equipment. There are trucks, jeeps, DUKWs, amphibious tanks, ambulances, wreckers, trailers, and halftracks in this August 23, 1944, view over Bagnoli harbor, along the coast from Pompeii.

Opposite, Above: *The view from Castel Sant'Elmo over the Teatro de San Carlo opera house and the Palazzo Reale de Napoli over toward the distinctive shoreline of Sorrento on August 15 as the fleet in Naples bay prepares to sail. In total 897 warships—284 British, French, and allied; 612 from the US—including 5 battleships, 20 cruisers, and 510 landing craft and landing ships were allocated to four attack forces: Alpha, Camel, Delta, and Sitka. Large numbers of landing craft also took part in the landings. Air cover and local close-support was provided by nine aircraft carriers (seven British and two US) under Rear-Adm Troubridge.*

Opposite, Below: *The complexities of any seaborne assault are easy to understand on a map, but everything is a lot more complicated on the ground. Keeping fire support channels clear for transports, landing on the assigned beaches at the assigned times, dropping paratroopers in the correct place: all of these prove difficult when weather and opposition come into play. As we'll see in the next chapter, the US airdrop was better than over Normandy but still had its problems. And as far as the beaches went, we'll also see how landing on Camel Sector's Red Beach wasn't possible and alternatives were sought.*

Right and Below Right: *Leaving nothing to chance—there were training areas in Africa and Italy which honed the amphibious landing skills of the assault divisions. The 36th and 45th trained at the Invasion Training Center at Salerno. The 3rd was at Pozzuoli on the Gulf of Naples and 1AATF at the Glider and Parachute School, Rome. There were full dress rehearsals on the night of August 7/8.*

lanning and executing an operation of the nature of Operation Dragoon was something the Allies were getting good at by August 1944. After its checkered on/off history, the real work on what was initially named Operation Anvil started in January 1944 by Force 163 in Algiers. Draft plans had been produced in 1943, but the number of divisions to be used, the airdrops, involvement of the French—all these things changed over the planning process.

Things began to come together once "Jumbo" Wilson had replaced Mark Clark, busy with the problematic Anzio landings, with "Sandy" Patch. With Patch at its helm, Seventh Army HQ made the final preparations for the invasion in Naples using men from his prior position as IV Corps commander. With him in Naples were the Western Naval Task Force and air force planners.

The plan was to land three infantry divisions—3rd, 36th, and 45th, all of which had experience of amphibious operations—with their attached tanks, tank destroyers, and artillery on beaches between Cavalaire and Agay. In the west, special forces would neutralize the batteries on the islands of Hyères, Port-Clos and Île du Levant, and French commandos would land at Cap Nègre. In the east, a smaller unit, 67 marines of the French Naval Assault Group would be put ashore. Behind the foreshore, paratroopers and glider forces would land near Le Muy and La Motte to seize high ground and ensure choke points from the beaches were kept open. There would be feint attacks by air and sea (towards Genoa, La Ciotat, and Antibes), as well as a pounding of fortifications and troop positions.

Once the beaches were secure, French II Corps—a combination of units from the French Expeditionary Force from Italy and North African troops—would come ashore.

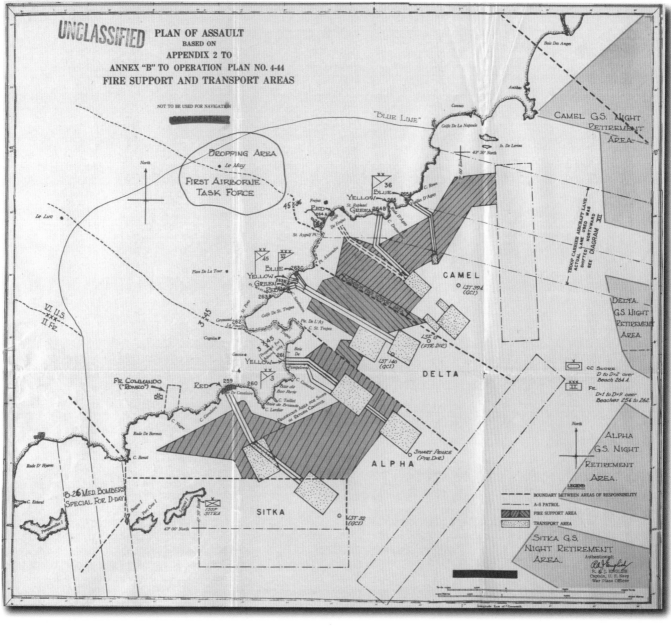

UNCLASSIFIED PLAN OF ASSAULT
BASED ON
APPENDIX 2 TO
ANNEX "B" TO OPERATION PLAN NO. 4-44
FIRE SUPPORT AND TRANSPORT AREAS

NOT TO BE USED FOR NAVIGATION

CONFIDENTIAL

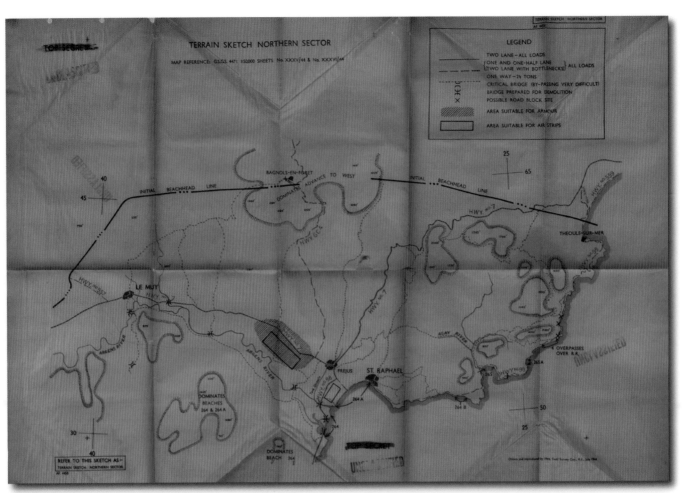

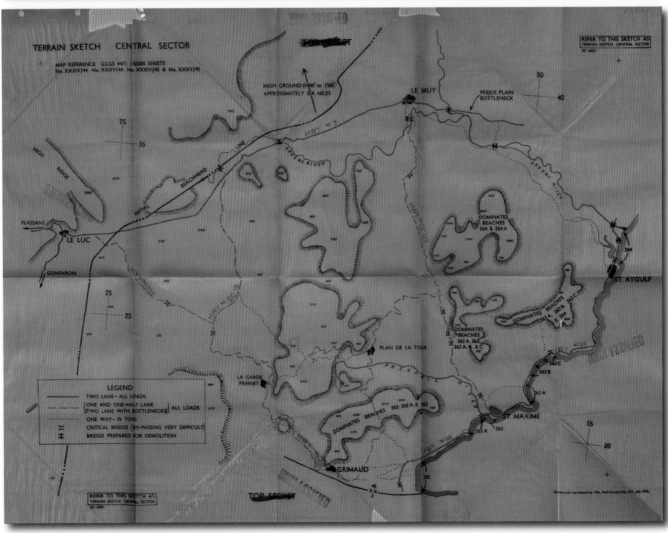

34

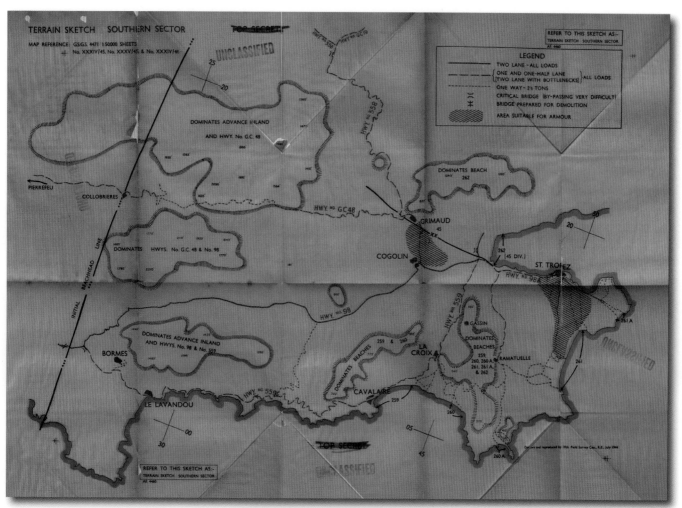

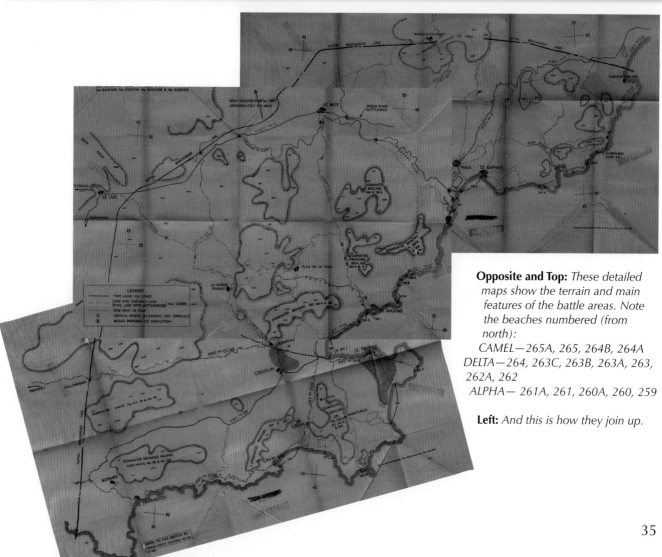

Opposite and Top: *These detailed maps show the terrain and main features of the battle areas. Note the beaches numbered (from north):*
CAMEL—265A, 265, 264B, 264A
DELTA—264, 263C, 263B, 263A, 263, 262A, 262
ALPHA— 261A, 261, 260A, 260, 259

Left: *And this is how they join up.*

Above: *Stakes in the fields that were potential landing grounds—Rommel's asparagus. Extremely effective, the dropping of paratroops before the gliders was meant to allow engineers to remove the stakes. This wasn't always possible and there were many crashes.*

Right: *Nearly 14,000 of the American Waco CG-4A glider were built and used in all the US Army's significant para operations. Smaller than the British Horsa, it could carry 13 men as opposed to 30—a significant difference when towing aircraft were so few.*

Left: *"Jumbo" Wilson visiting 2nd Independent Para Brigade HQ before the invasion. General Henry Maitland Wilson was Supreme Allied Commander in the Mediterranean, having succeeded Eisenhower in January 1944.*

Below Left: *2nd Independent Para Brigade receive their orders.*

Below: *There were three intended landing areas for paratroopers and gliders: DZ/LZ-A, DZ/LZ-O, and DZ-C. The British and American Paras were dropped to hold up enemy reinforcements so they wouldn't be able to reach the invasion beaches quickly and also to ensure the choke point around Le Muy was safely in Allied hands so that the advance west and north could start unhindered. In this task they were considerably assisted by the local Maquis—to an extent that was unexpected by the planners.*

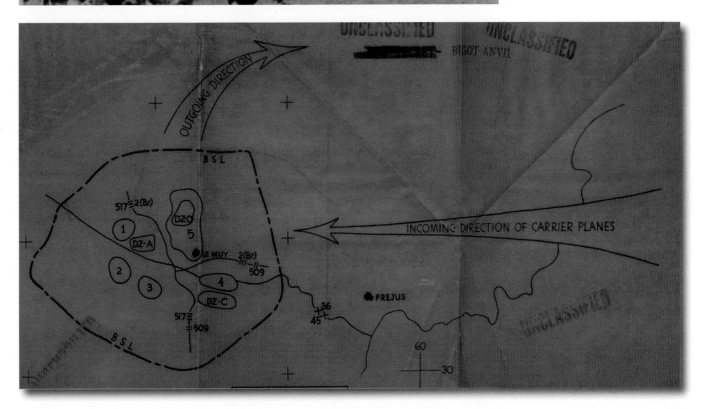

The Invasion of Elba

The invasion of Elba wasn't a military imperative. Indeed, the Allied advances in Italy meant that the island was no longer being used to screen the despatch of German reinforcements down the coast: strategically, it was a backwater. The commander of Allied Forces in Italy, General Sir Harold Alexander agreed. However, there was an important dissenter: Général de Lattre de Tassigny was convinced that an invasion would help train his men and also ensure that people in France could see that the French Army meant business. As a result, on June 17 Operation Brassard commenced. The French forces were commanded by Général Joseph Magnan whose unit, the 9e Division d'infanterie Coloniale loaded on Corsica. The landings were led by the French Bataillon de Choc and Commandos d'Afrique and RN commandos. The former's objectives were primarily gun batteries; the latter were tasked with neutralizing the German Flak ship *Köln* in Marino di Campo. *Köln*'s armament was a threat to the landing beaches. The preliminaries went well, but the German artillery wasn't silenced and accurate fire led to the arrival of the 9e Division over only one of the two designated beaches. While they waited for the French to clear the town, artillery ignited demolition charges and the ensuing explosion killed many of the RN commandos. In spite of this disaster, the Germans evacuated the island on the 20th. They left behind 500 dead and some 2,000 captured.

Opposite: *A German MG42 position well-placed to command the beaches.*

Above Left: *Classic view of a Goumier in Italy. Note the distinctive jellaba, a Moroccan cloak in brown with a grey stripe. The Goumiers fought in Tabors*

(battalions) and it was the 2e Groupe de Tabors Marocains that took part in the invasion of Elba. The Goumiers quickly picked up a reputation for being good fighters but dangerous to civilians, too. Many were executed for rape or sentenced to hard labor.

Above: *Troops disembarking on Elba.*

Below: *After initial resistance to the invasion, the garrison—Festungs-Bataillone 902 and 908, men of Marine-Artillerie-Abteilung 616 and others—slipped away on the evening of June 20.*

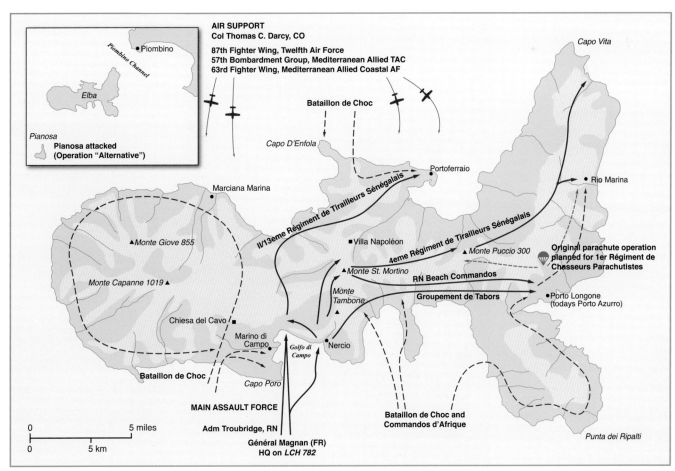

Embarkation

Control Force (Vice Adm Henry Kent Hewitt)
• Flagship USS *Catoctin*, destroyer and minesweepers

Special Operations Group (Capt H. C. Johnson)
• Western Diversionary Unit (Johnson) USS *Endicott*, PT boats, ASRCs, and minelayers
• Eastern Diversionary Unit (Lt Cdr Douglas Fairbanks, Jr) gunboats, PT boats, and minelayers

Task Force 84 Alpha Force (Rear Adm Frank J. Lowry)
• Force Flagship Group
• Assault Groups—Red Beach, Yellow Beach
• Gunfire Support Group
• Minesweeper Group
• Salvage and firefighting Group

Task Force 85 Delta Force (Rear Adm Bertram J. Rodgers)
• Force Flagship Group
• Transport Group
• Assault Groups—Red Beach, Green Beach, Yellow Beach, Blue Beach
• Gunfire Support Group
• Minesweeper Group
• Salvage and firefighting Group

Task Force 87 Camel Force (Rear Adm Spencer S. Lewis)
• Force Flagship Group
• Assault Groups—Red Beach, Green Beach, Yellow Beach, Blue Beach
• Bombardment Group
• Minesweeper Group
• Salvage and Firefighting Group

Task Force 86 Sitka Force (Rear Adm Lyal A. Davidson)
• Gunfire Support Group
• Transport Group
• Minesweeper Group

Task Force 88 Aircraft Carrier Force (Rear Adm Thomas Hope Troubridge, RN)

TG 80.6 AS and Convoy Control Group (Capt J. P. Clay)

1 *Four LSTs—(right to left) USS LST-178, USS LST-74, unidentified, and USS LST-656 load at Bagnoli, Italy, August 8, 1944.*

2 *US 3rd Infantry Division men (note the playing card logos on helmet backs) at Bagnoli harbor. USS LST-603, USS LST-74, and USS LST-141 are the vessels and the date is July 31, 1944, during an embarkation exercise prior to Operation Dragoon.*

3 *Another view of 3rd Division loading at Bagnoli, but this time it's for real. The date is August 8 and the loading for the invasion has begun.*

4 *An invasion convoy en route to Southern France, August 16, 1944. It includes two escort aircraft carriers, and an old British light cruiser (in left distance). The destroyer HMS Tuscan is at right.*

5 *US troops head toward the Riviera. Note the VI Corps identification and the 20mm weapons.*

2 THE AIRBORNE LANDINGS

THE LEAKIN DEACON

In the early morning of August 15, 1944, the skies over western Italy were filled with aircraft as the second invasion of France began. First to drop were three serials (a formation usually composed of several flights and separated from other formations in a mission by a specified time interval) of Pathfinders—nine C-47s—whose task was to set up beacons to guide in Mission Albatross: 396 C-47s dropping 5,607 men in ten serials. These were the British 2nd Independent Para Brigade's 4th, 5th and 6th Para Battalions on DZ-O, the 509th Battalion Combat Team (509th PIB, 463rd Para FA Bn) on DZ-C, and the 517th Regimental Combat Team (517th PIR, 460th Para FA Bn, and a platoon of 596th Engr Co) aimed for DZ-A.

As was typical of parachute operations in World War II, little went to plan. The Pathfinder aircraft encountered heavy fog and only those of the 2nd Ind Para Bde landed in the right area. With neither of their landing areas illuminated, the following US Paras were dropped on instrument navigation with mixed results. Half of the 509th landed correctly, the rest landed in Saint-Tropez. Sixteen men disappeared completely, almost certainly having been dropped over the sea.

Things were worse for the 517th. None landed on DZ-A. They were spread out from Lorgues in the west to Fréjus in the east. 3/517th landed around Fayence over 10 miles from DZ-A.

Next the British gliders of Mission Bluebird tried their luck. The persistent fog led to the recall of the Horsas but the Wacos came in with their precious artillery pieces. Subsequently, the Bluebird Horsas returned and landed that afternoon as did Mission Canary (551st PIB paratroopers), and Mission Dove (glider landings on LZ-O by the 550th PIB, a platoon of 887th Engr Co, 602nd FA Bn, and 887th Engr Co). There was considerable confusion as so many gliders landed and some casualties—17 killed and 158 wounded. Luckily, however, the operation was completed without interference from enemy aircraft and with very little Flak encountered at any stage.

But in spite of the problems, the airborne troops—with considerable assistance from the FFI—were causing chaos to the Germans with roadblocks and attacks on convoys and troop movements, and by the close of D-Day had taken Saint-Tropez, secured the area around La Motte, and made contact with the infantry from the beachheads.

Above: *This memorial is at Draguignan and remembers the meeting on August 16 between the US 551st Parachute Infantry Battalion and the Resistance. The 551st had been dropped over DZ-C on the 15th. On the 16th the FFI informed the task force HQ that it had taken Draguignan. The task force commander, Maj Gen Robert T. Frederick, sent a company of the 551st to Draguignan. After a short struggle the Germans surrendered and the 551st captured 800 men, the commander (Generalmajor Ludwig Bieringer) and HQ of the Draguignan Feldkommandanteur, and the HQ of LXII Army Corps. They also captured a fuel dump that would prove very useful.*

Below: *The flightpath and landing areas of the 1st Allied Airborne Task Force. The blue dots show navigation beacons.*

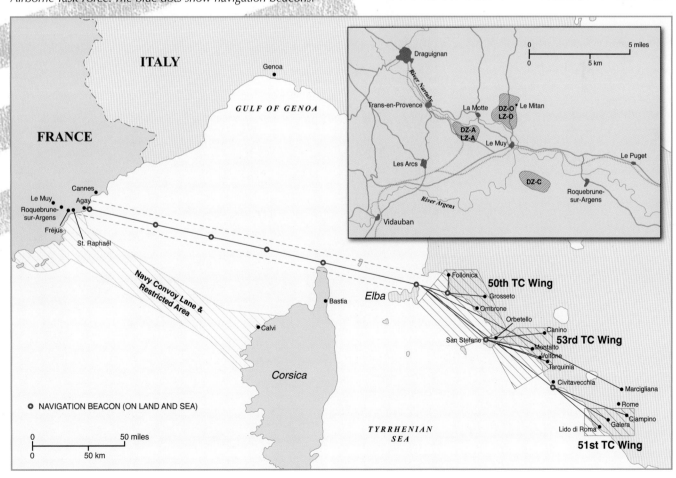

This spread: *It's the afternoon of August 14, 1944, and 1st Platoon A/517th PIR is readying itself at Canino airfield in Italy for the flight to southern France. The platoon was commanded by 1Lt Milton "Chopper" M. Kienlen (far right in above photo), and it will be carried in C-47 #2100548 of 438th Troop Carrier Group, part of 53rd TC Wing. The aircraft left Canino at 00:30 on August 15 and jumped over DZ-A at 04:32. Note their camouflage which has been sprayed over them. After dropping around Les Arcs, 1/517—who had set up its CP at Sainte-Rosaline—fought hard to take the town: this was effected finally when 3/517 arrived with heavy weapons.*

LE 15 AOÛT 1944
SAINTE ROSELINE
ET SA REGION
ÉTAIENT LIBÉRÉES A 4 HEURES DU MATIN
PAR LE 517e REGIMENT DE TROUPES AEROPORTÉES
AMERICAINES SOUS LES ORDRES DU COLONEL
RUPERT D. GRAVES

Paratroopers and glidermen are at their most vulnerable when landing, and don't have the heavy weapons to fight off armored counterattacks. The fighting at Arnhem, a month later, showed what could happen. Operation Dragoon's air landings, while less accurate than those at Arnhem, were not attacked by armor: 11. Panzer was still to the west of the Rhône. Helped by local FFI, the paras were able to cause great confusion in German ranks, and fortuitously encircled and then captured LXII Corps HQ and CG General der Infanterie Ferdinand Neuling.

The arrival of the gliders (these photos show the landings at the north end of LZ-O) and paratroopers on the afternoon of August 15 was planned to provide the men and equipment the Airborne Task Force needed to fulfill the primary mission: ensure that no German troops could affect the fighting on the coast. In fact, there was little attempt to to do so. 11. Panzer was too far from the front to achieve what 21. Panzer did in Normandy and the quality of the troops defending the coast was proved to be poor by the speed with which the three US divisions wrapped them up. There was some resistance in Le Muy, which didn't fall until D+1. The fighting around Les Arcs was also heavy. Nearly five miles from Le Muy, the German garrison had held out against attacks by the 517th and it was only the timely arrival of the 517th men who had landed around Fayence that saved a difficult situation. In the evening of the 15th they were assisted by elements of 180th RCT. Units of the 45th and the Airborne task force were able to hold off an attack by German 244. Infantry Division.

Below, inset Left to Right: *Memorials at Le Muy and La Motte remember the bravery of the liberators and the fact that La Motte was the first village liberated in Provence.*

Right: *Patrol of 517th. Scattered in the drop, the paratroopers caused confusion in German ranks. Unlike during Operation Market Garden where the German response was markedly tougher, there were few organized attempts to wipe out the paratroopers who were able—in conjunction, often, with the FFI—to accomplish most of their objectives.*

Below Right and Bottom: *Waco CG-4As at Le Muy. Note the stakes, many still standing.*

Opposite, Above and Below Left: *Around 10,000 men from the 1st Allied Airborne Task Force were delivered to France. Around 450 were killed, and 300 were wounded. This is the aid station at La Motte.*

Below Right: *Combat cameramen at Le Muy on August 17. These are S/Sgt Ed Peterson and Sgt Irving Leibowitz.*

2nd Independent Para Battalion

The first part of the operation went well: the Pathfinders of 2nd Independent Para Brigade were delivered exactly where they needed to be, a feat of dead reckoning navigation that left one of the team within 100 yards of the objective when all the land around was obscured by fog. By 04:30 the Eureka beacons were in place and at 04:54 the first serial dropped its troops through the fog using the Eureka beacon. The accuracy was almost perfect, as it was for many of the following serials, but there were a number—most of the 64th Group serials—that went astray and over 50 sticks were dropped in the wrong areas. Worse was to follow: the Horsas that were bringing the heavy weapons were also delayed by fog and didn't arrive until later that afternoon. In spite of these mishaps, the 2nd Brigade quickly secured the drop zone for future deliveries and occupied Le Mitan. One battalion took Clastron and made contact with the 517th at La Motte. However, the attack on Le Muy stalled at the bridge over the Nartuby and, without their heavy weapons, it fell to the 550th to complete the job the next day, after they failed in a night attack. On D+1 the British forces pushed north and east of Le Muy. They were relieved on the morning of the 18th by 36th Infantry Division. The brigade was released to return to other duties on the 2nd.

6 PARA BN RV.

2 PARA BDE GP. D.Z.

CLASTRON.

1 *Maj Gen Kenneth Crawford (right) with Brig Charles Pritchard—CO 2nd Para Brigade—Lt-Col Coken and Capt St Lawrence*

2 *British Paras watch the gliders coming in from the outskirts of La Motte.*

3 *Inside a British Horsa en route to France.*

4 *Aerial photograph of DZ-O (1) and LZ-O (2). La Motte is at 3; Le Mitan is off the map at 4; Le Muy is off the map at 5. 6 is the main road, the D47, which runs from Trans-en-Provence to Bagnols-en-Forêt.*

5 and 6 *Two views of DZ-O showing a Waco glider named Annabelle that is slightly the worse for wear. In 5 there is a British LMG (Bren) team; in both images a Waco can be seen circling.*

IN MEMORIAM
AUGUST 1944
A LA MÉMOIRE DES SOLDATS
DE LA FIRST SPÉCIAL SERVICE
FORCE TOMBÉS EN PROVENCE

IN MEMORY OF THE SOLDIERS
OF THE FIRST SPECIAL SERVICE
FORCE FALLEN ON THE
PROVENCE COUNTRY

1 *British 2nd Brigade and US men of the 509th PIB take a break at La Mitan.*

2 *The First Special Service Force was—as the insignia identifies—a combined US and Canadian unit from which the special forces of both countries trace their lineage. In 2013 the unit was awarded the Congressional Gold Medal.*

3 *British and American troops confer at Le Mesle.*

4 *Battle-weary men of B/509th PIB on the D47 north of Le Muy.*

5 and 6 *Le Muy was taken by men of the 517th PIR. Little has changed in the town center.*

7 *British Paras await their return to Italy.*

Below: *The First Special Service Force and the 1st Airborne Task Force were given the task of liberating the Riviera to the Italian border—the Champagne Campaign as it was dubbed—ULTRA having identified that the Germans were retreating pell-mell back to the safety of Italy. By August 26 they had reached the Var. Nice fell on August 30 and C/509th PIB, led by Capt Jessie Walls, cleared Monaco (a neutral state) of Germans. By September 7 the Italian border was reached. At this point, the advance was halted. The border would remain the front line, protected by minefields on both sides, until the end of the war, fiercely defended by the Germans.*

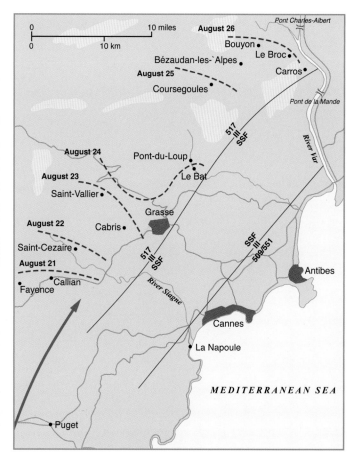

3 THE SEABORNE LANDINGS

The troops leave the beaches and head inland. Fires and smoke are still visible in the background.

The invasion took place on August 15, 1944. There were nearly 900 warships (including 254 British and Allied; 31 French; 7 Greek; 612 USA) allocated across the four attack forces and, in addition, over 1,370 ship-borne assault landing craft. Air cover and support was provided by Rear-Adm Troubridge with seven British and two US escort carriers. After intensive air and sea bombardments, the Allies used Apex drone landing craft to explode underwater mine defenses. These worked quite well, although not on the planned 14:00 Camel Red assault where enemy shelling and the failure of the drones led to the landings there being canceled. The troops went ashore over Camel Green at 15:15. Dummy paratroops were dropped northwest of Toulon and a simulated landing was made at La Ciotat Bay to confuse the enemy.

The attack on the Îles d'Hyères—Port Cros and Levant—by the Sitka attack force (1SSF and French Commandos d'Afrique) were successful; although the "battery" on the islands was a dummy. By 10:00 the French Commandos had taken the high ground and the battery. Unfortunately, in the east, the small French Naval Assault Force was trapped in a minefield and forced to surrender.

The three main landing areas saw three experienced US infantry divisions—3rd, 36th, and 45th—encounter light resistance, although Saint-Raphaël and Le Muy each held out for a while. By the close of D+1, the US forces had reached their initial objective—the "Blue Line."

MAIN OPERATION DRAGOON CONVOYS

Route 1 from Naples

August 9: SS-1, SS-1A, and SS-1B assault convoys (of 145 LCTs and other ships) leave for staging port Ajaccio

August 11: Sitka assault convoy SY-1 leaves for Propriano

August 12: Assault convoys SF-2, SF-2A, and SF-2B (115 LCTs and 30 other vessels) depart for Ajaccio
Assault convoys SM-1, SM-1A, and SM-1B depart
Sitka gunfire support group departs to Corsica then along Route 10

August 13: Combat loader convoy departs
Merchant vessel convoys SF-1, SM-2 departs

Route 2 from Brindisi and Taranto

August 10: Convoy TM-1 departs Taranto

August 11: Delta gunfire support group departs Taranto joined by French vessels off Bizerte

August 12: Aircraft carrier force (7 RN and 2 USN carriers) departs Malta and joins Route 2
Personnel ship convoy TF-1 departs Taranto

August 13: Alpha gunfire support group departs Malta and joins Route 2

Route 3 from Oran

August 10: Convoy AM-1 leaves

August 11: Convoy Special No. 2 leaves

Route 6 from Palermo

August 13: Camel gunfire support group departs

August 14: Convoy Special No. 1 (tankers) departs for Ajaccio on a shuttle run

Route 9 from Corsica

August 13: Convoy SS-1, SS-1A, SS-1B departs Ajaccio for assault

August 14: Convoy SY-1 departs Propriano to rendezvous with Sitka gunfire support group
LCI convoy SF-2, SF-2A, SF-2B depart Ajaccio for assault area
First part Eastern diversion force departs Ajaccio; second part departs Calvi—they rendezvous and proceed
First and second parts Western diversion force depart Calvi—rendezvous and proceed

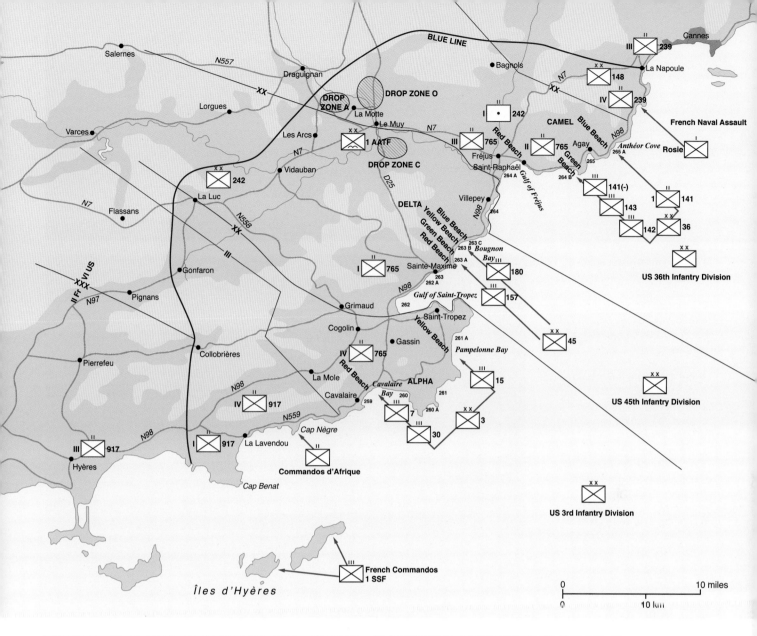

Salernes •   N557   Draguignan •   BLUE LINE   Bagnols •   Cannes

XX   DROP ZONE O

III ⊠ 239   La Napoule

XX ⊠ 148   N7

Lorgues •   DROP ZONE A   La Motte   I ⊡ 242   XX   IV ⊠ 239

Varces •   Les Arcs •   Le Muy •   N7   CAMEL   Blue Beach   French Naval Assault

XX ⊠ 1 AATF   III ⊠ 765   II ⊠ 765   Agay   Anthéor Cove   I ⊠ Rosie

Vidauban •   DROP ZONE C   Fréjus   Saint-Raphaël   265 A   265

D25   264 A   Gulf of Fréjus   Green Beach   264 B

XX ⊠ 242   DELTA   Villepey   III ⊠ 141(-)   II ⊠ 141

La Luc •   N558   264   III ⊠ 143   1

Flassans •   N7   XX   Blue Beach   Yellow Beach   Green Beach   Red Beach   III ⊠ 142   XX ⊠ 36

263 C   263 B   Bougnon Bay   US 36th Infantry Division

Gonfaron •   I ⊠ 765   Sainte-Maxime   263 A   III ⊠ 180

XXX VI US   II Fr   III   263   262 A

N97   Pignans •   Grimaud •   N98   262   Gulf of Saint-Tropez   III ⊠ 157

Cogolin •   Saint-Tropez   Yellow Beach   XX ⊠ 45   US 45th Infantry Division

Pierrefeu •   Collobrières •   Gassin •   261 A   Pampelonne Bay

IV ⊠ 765   La Mole •   Red Beach   ALPHA   III ⊠ 15   261

IV ⊠ 917   Cavalaire •   Cavalaire Bay   260   261   XX ⊠ 3   US 3rd Infantry Division

N559   259   260 A   III ⊠ 7   III ⊠ 30

III ⊠ 917   Hyères   N98   Cap Nègre   La Lavendou •   II ⊠ Commandos d'Afrique

I ⊠ 917   Cap Benat

Îles d'Hyères   III ⊠ French Commandos 1 SSF

0   10 miles   0   10 km

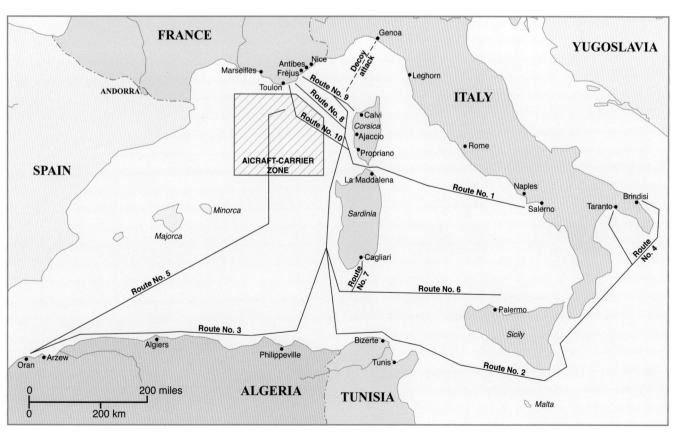

FRANCE   Genoa   YUGOSLAVIA

ANDORRA   Marseilles •   Antibes • Nice   Fréjus   Decoy attack   Leghorn •   ITALY

SPAIN   Toulon   Route No. 9   Route No. 8   Route No. 10   Calvi •   Corsica   Ajaccio •   Rome •

AICRAFT-CARRIER ZONE   Proprilano •   La Maddalena •   Route No. 1   Naples •

Minorca   Sardinia   Salerno •   Taranto •   Brindisi •

Majorca   Route No. 4

Cagliari •   Route No. 7   Route No. 6

Route No. 5   Palermo •

Route No. 3   Bizerte •   Sicily

Oran •   Arzew •   Algiers •   Philippeville •   Tunis •   Route No. 2   Malta

0   200 miles   0   200 km   ALGERIA   TUNISIA

1 *A Chevrolet medical truck broken down on the beach.*

2 *A Dodge WC54 ambulance is ferried towards the beach. Note the caduceus badge near driver's window.*

3 **and** 4 *Alpha Yellow, August 15. Note US Navy SP (Shore Patrol) armband (3) and stretcher bearers (4) behind improvised sand protection.*

5 *A DUKW carries blood and medical personnel on a landing beach on August 26.*

6 *Landing craft were used for beach evacuation of wounded.*

The Medics

Dealing with casualties, evacuating them back to hospitals in the rear, and ensuring sufficient medical supplies—these are important military functions and the US Army was very good at them. Seventh Army's medical section had been reduced as its men were siphoned off to fight in Italy. However, the skeleton staff left behind were split in early 1944 between Force 163 where the operational planning was taking place, and Oran where US supply organization was based. By June the army's staff had expanded and was run by Col Myron P. Rudolph. As elsewhere, the navy was responsible for shipboard medical care and the army from the high-water mark on the beaches. Each of the combat divisions had its own organic medical battalion and medical detachments; each RCT was supported during the landings by a collecting company and clearing platoon. 1AATF was supported by a collecting company with clearing elements. The assault divisions each had two field hospital platoons. Attached to these were surgeons and specialists from 2nd Auxiliary Surgical Group. There were three separate medical battalions initially attached to beach groups to deal with casualties. Evacuation was by landing craft or water ambulance. The French divisions has similar medical arrangements. Between D+1 and D+4 each of the divisions would see its own 400-bed evacuation hospital; two others staffed by the French would accompany them. Two hospital ships arrived on D+1, with others available to arrive on a daily basis up to D+10. In reality, things didn't go according to plan. There were delays in getting manpower and equipment into position on the beaches—but it didn't matter. As the official history says, "Delays ... might been serious had casualties been heavier than they were. ... Hospital admissions, including admissions to clearing stations, for the beach phase of the operation were approx. 3,000."

Alpha Beaches

The Alpha Beaches stretched from just south of Saint-Tropez (Pampelonne Beach) west to Cavalaire. US 3rd Infantry Division landed here, the 7th followed by the 30th RCTs at Cavalaire and the 15th RCT at Pampelonne. The opposition was IV/Grenadier-Regiment 765. The defenders—many Osttruppen—didn't put up much of a defense and the main casualties were from mines: two landing craft from Co G/7th Infantry and another LCVP of Co F hit mines and sustained some 60 casualties. In spite of this 3rd Infantry Division advanced rapidly and had cleared the beach area by midafternoon, striking inland to fulfill its mission assignments: to capture Saint-Tropez, Grimaud, and Cogolin; to clear the Saint-Tropez peninsula; to advance inland aggressively and destroy all enemy resistance it encountered.

Above: Troops come ashore on Alpha Red near Cavalaire. These LCI(L)s are from the sixth wave.

Right and Opposite, Bottom: It's not surprising that Saint-Tropez has gained a name for being a rich playground in recent years. In 1944 there are fewer "gin palaces" in the harbor and rather more smoke from battle. Starus/WikiCommons (CC BY-SA 3.0)

Above Left: *Red Beach area, France. A mine explodes near shore. The use of Apex drones was successful on Alpha beaches: as the Engineers war history says, of the 18 used, "15 drones destroyed as many obstacles, but 2 circled aimlessly, and 1 roared back into the fleet area, damaging a sub-chaser when it blew up."*

Above: *Liberation Memorial at the port of Cavalaire-sur-Mer. Next to it a memorial remembers 3rd Division.* Villy Fink Isaksen/ WikiCommons (CC BY-SA 4.0)

Left: *Beach defenses at Cavalaire. There was a battery of six 155mm guns near Saint-Tropez, manned by 1/HKAR 1291.*

Left: *Allied shipping unloading in Cavalaire Bay on August 18.*

Opposite Center: *Pampelonne Beach.*

Opposite, Below: *Both 3rd Infantry Division attacks were spearheaded by DD tanks from A Company 756th Tank Battalion. One struck a mine and was disabled.*

Left: *DUKWs did the legwork ferrying equipment ashore from the transports—here on Alpha Red. Note transports offshore, with barrage balloons overhead.*

Below: *Landing on the beach at Pampelonne on August 15, these men had sailed from Naples on the USS Samuel Chase a veteran LCVP which had already seen action during Operations Torch, Husky, Avalanche, and Neptune, and would go on (after an overhaul) to the Pacific. Note the beach markers (red and black) which identified landing locations, beach exits, etc. The US Beach battalions, headed by a Beachmaster, were tasked with preparing the beach for all the various personnel who would be landing—initially, the medical teams. The Beach battalions surveyed the beach to identify the best landing areas and exits, and set up communications with the fleet and the assault troops using radios or other signaling equipment.*

Above: *Pampelonne Bay provides a beautiful sandy beach which is perfect for an invading force. Sparsely defended, it was taken easily. Its primary problem, however, is that it has poor exit roads. After D+5 it wasn't used for unloading.*

Right: *LCI(L)-674 unloading at around 08:43 on Alpha's Yellow Beach. Visible are men of 2/36th Engineers.*

Below Right: *The immediate objective of 3rd Infantry Division was to clear the Saint-Tropez peninsula. Note the elements of 509th PIB misdropped in the area.*

Saint-Tropez

Opposite: *Men of B and C Cos 509th PIR and of 463rd PFAB landed off course near Saint-Tropez. Led by Captain Jess Walls they advanced into the town making contact with FFI troops of the Maures Group led by Marc Rainaud, an architect. The German garrison retreated into the citadel but later that day surrendered. The US paratroops lost 22 men in the process if you include 17 of B/509th who died when dropped over water. The photographs show: **1** Marc Rainaut, Mlle Nicola Celebono-vitch, and Pvt Winfred D. Eason after the battle; **2** Marc Rainaut receiving the Silver Star from General Patch; **3** Seventh Army (note shoulder patches) medics and FFI look through discarded weapons. The rifle is a German Kar98k.*

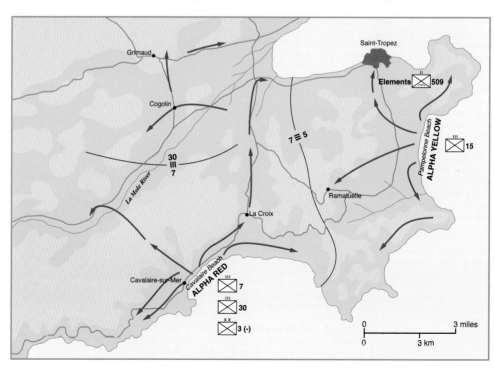

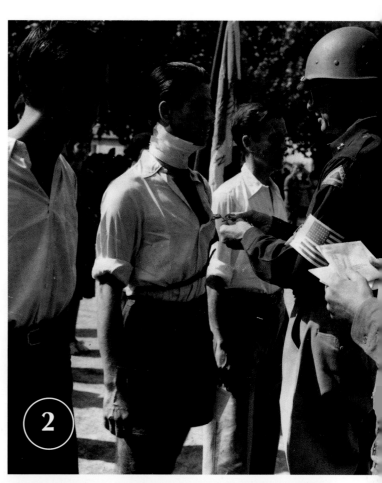

Above: *Memorial on Pampelonne beach.*

Above Right and Right: *The gulf of Saint-Tropez is an excellent harbor. General Patch chose Saint-Tropez as his HQ and it was here that he met General de Lattre de Tassigny early on the 19th and gave the French general permission to attack Toulon before he had built up his forces. De Lattre argued that this would take ten days and give the Germans time to bring in reserves.*

Below: *Today the gulf of Saint-Tropez is used for cruise ships. This view looks over to Sainte-Maxime. Delta Beach is around Pointe des Sardinaux, on the right.*

Above Left: *Memorial at Saint-Tropez remembering the landings.*

Left: *View over Saint-Tropez towards Pampelonne Beach.* Starus/WikiCommons (CC BY-SA 3.0)

Above: *The Saint-Tropez citadel in which the German garrison holed up. Beneath it is a memorial to the US paratroopers of B/509th PIR who died when dropped into the sea.* Remi Jouan/WikiCommons (CC BY-SA 3.0)

71

Delta Beaches

Manned by I/Grenadier-Regiment 765, the defenses around the Sainte-Maxime area included a naval battery but few beach obstacles, although mines accounted for four DD tanks on Delta Blue. The 180th landed there and on Delta Yellow. The 157th landed on Red and Green and both regiments had a harder task ahead of them: the 157th in Sainte-Maxime and the 180th in Saint-Aygulf. Inland there was also resistance, but the 45th Recon Troop was able to meet up with 1AATF at Le Muy. Later in the day tanks were sent to help 509th PIR take the town. The 179th Regiment was landed in the afternoon.

1 Beach 263A, La Nartelle South seen during the invasion.

2 View over Sainte-Maxime toward Saint-Tropez. Note the bridge over the River Préconil at **1**.

3 USS LCI-513 and LCT-1143 unloading. Note the use of metal roadway on the beach.

4 LST-996, identified in its caption as the first LST to reach Delta beach. Note the two anti-aircraft positions.

6 Men of 157th Infantry head toward Sainte-Maxime where they will face a tough battle and have to call in naval gun support.

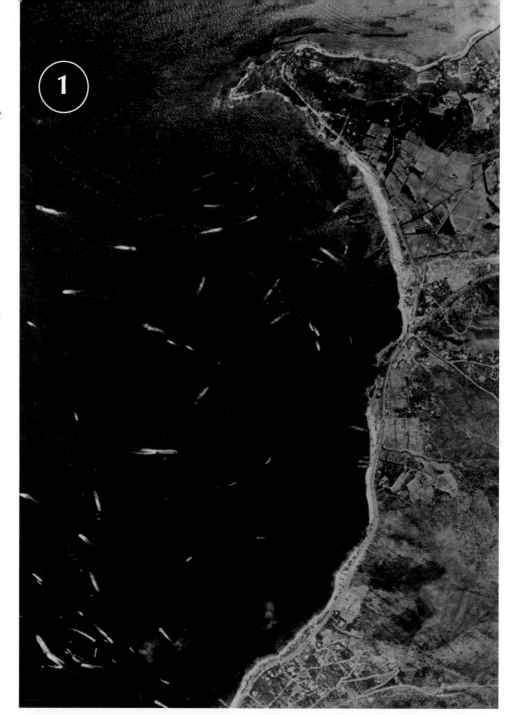

1 Two LCI(L)s—522 (left) and 552—on Delta Red. This is the 45th Division's Medical Battalion coming ashore. Casualties were light on the Delta beaches,

2 An LCT heads towards Delta Yellow. The troops onboard don't look concerned about gunfire so it is a later wave.

3 USS Catoctin (AGC-5) was the force flagship for Operation Dragoon. Launched in January 1943 as SS Mary Whitridge, she was converted and sent Algiers where she became flagship for Commander, 8th Fleet on March 19. Visited by King George VI on July 24 at Naples, she sailed toward the invasion beaches on August 13. On board were Secretary of the Navy James Forrestal and the commanders of US Seventh Army, VI Corps, Twelfth Air Force, and French Naval Forces. "Shamrock," as she was codenamed, had a crew of around 50 officers and 550 men, six of whom were killed and 31 wounded during a German air raid on the 18th. Catoctin was armed with two 5-inch, four paired 40mm, and ten paired 20mm guns. Note the SK-1 air search radar.

4 DUKWs arriving on Delta Yellow.

5 Coming into Red Beach, along-side LCI(L)-522—the same ship as seen in photo 1. Note the concrete antitank wall at the back of the beach. It was eight feet high and needed a hole to be blown in it by the engineers.

6 A German machine-gun team killed during the fighting in Sainte-Maxime.

Camel Beaches

The most easterly of the three landing areas, Camel sector was the area where the attackers came closest to having a problem on August 15, but quick-thinking, flexibility, and professionalism ensured that there were no slipups. The attack was prosecuted by 36th Infantry Division led by Maj Gen John E. Dahlquist, the only one of the divisional commanders who was an unknown quantity to VI Corps CG Maj Gen Lucian K. Truscott, Jr. As the eastern-most division, the 36th was tasked with keeping the flank of the operation secure, at the same time securing the port of Saint-Raphaël and the tempting beach 264A. The Germans were well aware that this was a good spot for the invasion troops to land, and had made provision for this: gun emplacements enfiladed the beach; there were beach obstacles aplenty, mines, and a number of interlocked strongpoints. There were three beaches in the sector: Blue (264C), Green (264B), and Red (264A). There were no problems on Green and Blue, but Red threatened to be a disaster, as the minesweepers sent to sweep the route in came under heavy fire. After bombing raids, attempts to clear a path using drones, and use of rocket salvoes all proved ineffective, the assault commander decided to switch the landings of 142nd Infantry Regiment to Camel Green. This was accomplished without problems, although it knocked the schedule out of kilter for a while. Once landed, the three infantry regiments proceeded with their missions: the 141st securing the eastern sector and heading up the road to Nice; the 143rd to take Saint-Raphaël and Fréjus; and the 142nd to head inland. On the 15th the 8th Beach Battalion opened Camel Yellow Beach—the Rade d'Agay—for traffic. It and Green were closed after D+4 by which time Camel Red and the port of Saint-Raphaël were in use.

Above Right: Results of shelling by USS Brooklyn (CL-40) on the German Flak positions near Cap Dramont, as photographed from one of Brooklyn's floatplanes.

Center and Below Right: Elements of the 141st and 143rd Infantry Regiments landed first at Dramont Bay (Camel Green) followed in the afternoon of the 15th by 142nd Infantry.

Above: *The 636th TD Bn leaving Camel Beaches on D-Day. There were three TD battalions involved in the campaign: the 601st, 636th, and 645th. The 636th had fought in Italy and elements joined TF Butler advancing through Draguignan to Grenoble. The 636th was also the first US unit to enter Lyon.*

Right: *The Third Reich spent a great deal of time and money on the development of cutting edge weaponry that made little difference to the outcome of the war, and may have been better spent elsewhere. However, the Henschel Hs293 radio-controlled anti-ship guided missile performed well, sinking a number of capital ships and—as seen here—leaving USS LST-282 burned out off Cap Dramont. The Allies, however, were working on the problem and thanks to the capture of an intact bomb and the radio-control elements in a Heinkel He 177, jamming rendered it less effective. The Allies' own "secret weapon," the Apex drones, were ineffective on Camel Red. Of the 10 launched, "Three wrecked some mined tetrahedrons, one exploded ... two ran up onto the sand, and one made tight circles offshore. A destroyer blew another out of the water when it veered seaward and sailors gingerly boarded the last two wayward robots to put them out of action." There is some speculation that German jamming may have affected the drones' performance.*

Right: *Memorial above Dramont Beach to Admiral Hewitt and the landings. The 36th Infantry Division who assaulted in the Camel sector had had a difficult 1944, having incurred severe losses at both Salerno and crossing the Rapido. They were unlucky again with Camel Red Beach, but their assault and subsequent advance showed the "Texans" fighting ability— and the decision to land at Cap Dramont kept the casualties down.*

Below Right and Below: *This is a classic view of Green Beach with Cap Dramont at left and the castle of the Île d'Or in the background (it is a modern folly). The M4A1 DD of 753rd Tank Battalion was immobilized during the landings. The caption identifies this tank as the first on the beach having been hit by a German shell. It knocked out machine gun nests on the beach but then the motor died—and later two feet of water was found inside the vehicle. In the background, bulldozers clear paths for vehicles coming in to land.*

CEST SUR CETTE PLAGE OPINIÂTREMENT

DÉFENDUE QUE, LE 15 AOÛT 1944,

DÉBARQUÈRENT EN FORCE LES HOMMES

DE LA 36ᵉ DIVISION D'INFANTERIE

AMÉRICAINE. C'EST D'ICI QU'AVEC LEURS

ALLIÉS FRANÇAIS ILS COMMENCÈRENT

LA POUSSÉE QUI LES MENA À TRAVERS

LA FRANCE, L'ALLEMAGNE ET L'AUTRICHE,

ACHEVANT LA DESTRUCTION COMPLÈTE DE

L'ARMÉE ALLEMANDE ET DU RÉGIME NAZI.

Above and Left: *The seventieth anniversary of the landings saw this memorial created. It includes a landing craft numbered LST-282. Hit by a Hs293 guided missile (see page 77), the commanding officer, Lt Lawrence E. Gilbert, was awarded the Naval Cross for saving the lives of a wounded signalman and, in the water, another helpless man.*

Below: *540th Engineer Combat Regiment DUKWs are downloaded from LCT1041 and LCT785—part of the fifth wave. The combat engineers and beach groups were hugely important in this—and every other— amphibious assault, reaching the beaches early, and having to contend with mines and booby traps. For example, 540th Beach Group "lost nearly a platoon when the detonation of one booby-trapped block killed four and wounded 27 men."*

Saint-Raphaël

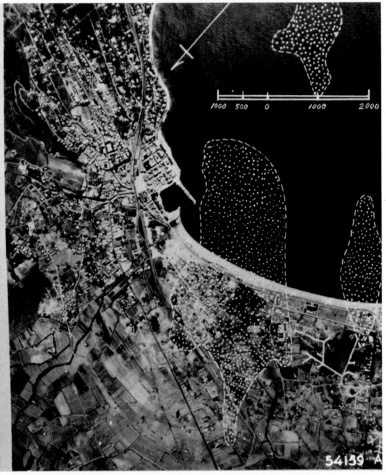

Opposite: *Saint-Raphaël beach (also seen above) was the best in the area with the best communications and access into the interior along the Argens valley. Unsurprisingly, it was well protected with 88mm antitank guns locally and a number of batteries of artillery in the surrounding hills. The infantry was elements of II/Grenadier-Regiment 765 and they saw off the original landing attempt in spite of bombing runs and naval bombardment. The Texans cleared Saint-Raphaël by 09.30 on D+1 but were held up along Camel Red, and the area wasn't cleared until midafternoon after fierce fighting.*

Above: *LCTs and LCMs landing supplies on Camel Red on D+5. LCTs present include LCT-198 and LCT-559. Note the matted ramp in foreground for DUKWs.*

Below Left: *Landings memorial in Saint-Raphaël. VI Corps commander Lucien Truscott was later critical of the decision to redirect troops bound for Camel Red. The heavy fighting there on D+1 shows that casualties would have been heavy—much more than the actual figures (in total five wounded).*

Below: *PzKpfw II turret mounted on the front at Saint-Raphaël.*

Above and Below: *One of the pillboxes that guarded the road and bridge into Saint-Raphaël. Today the pillboxes have gone*

Opposite: *Saint-Raphaël then and now. Note construction equipment (at right, **bottom**) clearing the worst debris in the afternoon of D+2.*

At the end of D+1 Patch and Truscott had a number of reasons to be thankful. First, the landings had gone much more easily than could have been predicted. Apart from some problems with the air missions, the seaborne side of things had not just proceeded well, but had seen objectives reached ahead of schedule. The seaborne divisions had met up with the airborne troops and—serendipitously—had advanced to Draguignan and netted General Bieringer, the military governor of the Var. Better still, intelligence reported no obvious buildup of German forces to allow for a serious counterattack.

Main photo: *The Armée d'Afrique fought well in France in spite of logistical problems. Here 3e DIA heads up toward Rupt.*

Inset: *The Rhin et Danube insignia was created after the liberation of Colmar. The idea for the image was Gérard Ambroselli's. He had been de Lattre's aide-de-camp in 1940 and had rejoined the general in Algiers in 1943. Colmar had conferred on First Army the right to bear the coat of arms of the city (red and green shield with a gold mace). Ambroselli added the waves to symbolize the rivers and the arrival of the army in Provence. The insignia was worn proudly by all who served in First Army.*

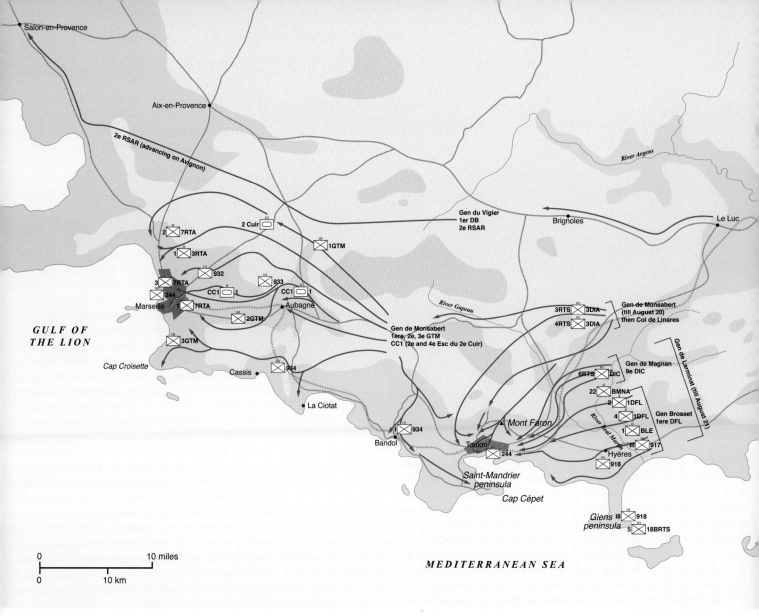

The map shows the following labels:

Salon-en-Provence

Aix-en-Provence

2e RSAR (advancing on Avignon)

River Argens

Le Luc

Gen du Vigier
1er DB
2e RSAR

Brignoles

2 | 7RTA

2 Cuir

1GTM

1 | 3RTA

932

3 | 7RTA

933

244

CC1 | 1

CC1 | 1

Marseille

1 | 7RTA

2GTM

Aubagne

River Gapeau

3RTS | 3DIA

Gen de Monsabert
(till August 20)
then Col de Linares

GULF OF
THE LION

3GTM

4RTS | 3DIA

Gen de Monsabert
1ere, 2e, 3e GTM
CC1 (2e and 4e Esc du 2e Cuir)

Cap Croisette

Cassis

934

Gen de Magnan
9e DIC

Gen de Larminat (till August 21)

La Ciotat

6RTS | DIC

22 | BMNA

2 | 1DFL

Mont Faron

4 | 1DFL

Gen Brosset
1ere DFL

934

Bandol

River Real Martin

1 | BLE

Toulon

917

244

Hyères

918

Saint-Mandrier
peninsula

Cap Cépet

Giens
peninsula

18 | 918

5 | 18BRTS

MEDITERRANEAN SEA

0 ——— 10 miles

0 ——— 10 km

Above: *The French advance on Toulon and Marseille. What we would today call the "coalition" of French and US Army forces that would make up Sixth Army Group after it became operational worked well in general but there were issues. Mainly equipped by the Americans, the French were short on engineers and logistics staff. They also had a political agenda that was different to that of the long-suffering commander of Sixth Army Group, Lt Gen Jacob L. Devers, whose patience and tolerance did much to make the partnership successful. De Lattre had to obey his political master—de Gaulle—and so at times was speaking for France rather than as commander of French Armée B or First Army as it became. And this meant that de Lattre disobeyed orders— for example in the defense of Strasbourg—and was certainly thought of by the senior American commanders as a "politico."*

The French Army has a long and proud history and remembers victories such as Castillon (1453), Fontenoy (1745), Austerlitz (1805), and Verdun (1916), but there can be few more satisfying than the taking of Toulon and Marseille by Armée B in August 1944.

It was the third time Général de Lattre had fought the Germans in metropolitan France during the war. He had fought against them when they invaded northern France in 1940. Then, as commander of 16th Military Division in Montpellier, he had fought again when they invaded Vichy France's Free Zone. This time he was the invader, returning to France after his escape from a Vichy prison in September 1943.

The French Army's involvement in Operation Dragoon had started with special forces commando operations on August 15. Next came Général Sudre's Combat Command 1 (CC1), which was attached to US VI Corps and was planned for use as its mobile armored force. In fact, after three days it returned to de Lattre's command—much against Truscott's wishes. One of the reasons for this is that the French forces had started to arrive at Saint-Tropez much more quickly than expected—thanks primarily to the lack of German opposition. De Lattre proposed to Patch that rather than wait for all his men, his army should move at once for Toulon before the Germans had a chance to reorganize.

De Lattre remembers, "only a fraction of the first echelon—that is, 16,000 men, 30 tanks, 80 medium guns—was on the spot ... to wait for the second echelon would involve a wait of from eight to ten days. ... But I still had to get authority to begin, and General Patch alone could give it to me ... It was after midday [on the 19th] when, by sheer insistence, I succeeded in overcoming the opposition of the cautious. General Patch gave me a free hand, the munitions, and my CC1." De Lattre sprang to action.

FRENCH ARMÉE B
Commander: Gén d'armée Jean de Lattre de Tassigny

II Corps d'Armée
(CO: Général Edgard de Larminat
   (replaced August 21)

**1re Division de marche
d'infanterie (DMI)***
(CO: Gén de div Diego Brousset)
1ère Brigade d'infanterie
2e Brigade d'infanterie
4e Brigade d'infanterie
1er Régiment d'artillerie (RA)
*1er Régiment de fusiliers-marins
   (reconnaissance regiment)*
8e Régiment de chasseurs d'Afrique

* **usually known by its original name
   1ère Division Française Libre (DFL)**

1re Division Blindée (DB)
(CO: Gén de div Jean Touzet du Vigier)
2e Régiment cuirassiers (RC)
2e Régiment de chasseurs d'Afrique (RCA)
5e Régiment de chasseurs d'Afrique
1er Bataillon de zouaves (BZ)
68e Régiment d'artillerie d'Afrique (RCA)

**3e Division d'infanterie
   Algeriénne (DIA)**
(CO: Gén de div Joseph de Goislard de
   Monsabert)
3e Régiment de tirailleurs Algériens (RTA)
7e Régiment de tirailleurs Algériens
4e Régiment de tirailleurs Tunisiens (RTT)
67e Régiment d'artillerie d'Afrique
*3e Régiment de spahis Algériens de
   reconnaissance (RSAR)*
Bataillon de Choc

**9e Division d'infanterie Coloniale
   (DIC)**
(CO: Gén de div Joseph Abraham
   Magnan)
4e Régiment de tirailleurs Sénégalais (RTS)
6e Régiment de tirailleurs Sénégalais
13e Régiment de tirailleurs Sénégalais
*Régiment d'artillerie colonial du Maroc
   (RACM)*
*Régiment d'infanterie colonial du Maroc
   (RICM)*
*Régiment colonial de chasseurs de chars
   (RCCC*
Groupe de commandos d'Afrique

**Auxilaire Feminin de l'Armée de
   Terre (AFAT)**
*5,000 secretaries, assistants, telephonists,
   radio operators, nurses, drivers*

Below: *"We had to be patient for a whole day, but on the 16th, at 17:00, the moment we had feverishly awaited at last arrived ... While the colors were hoisted, the Marseillaise broke out from all ships as with one voice ... In the luminous splendor of a Provençal summer evening ... The convoy slowly advanced across a sea that was alight with golden reflections and was without a ripple. ... The landing began at once. The 1DFL took the Sylvabelle beach, the 3e DIA, the army HQ, and the CC2 took the La Foux beach at the far end of Saint-Tropez bay."* As they arrived the Luftwaffe bombed the area and the French took 80 casualties. This photo shows men of 3e DIA.

The Army of Africa (Armée d'Afrique)

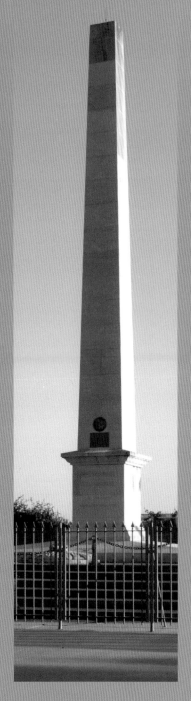

Above: *The Armée d'Afrique is celebrated in Saint-Raphaël with this fine column.*

The antecedents of the French Army of Africa were the French settlers of North Africa—the *Zouaves* (light infantry) and *Chasseurs d'Afrique* (light cavalry)—and the irregular Arab and Berber units—*Spahis* (light cavalry), *Goumiers* (specialist night and mountain troops) and *Tirailleurs* (sharpshooters/infantry) from Algeria, Tunisia, and Morocco recruited by the early French colonial forces during their conquest of the Mahgreb. Commanded by French Army officers, they were formally incorporated into the French Army as the XIX Army Corps in 1873 and although used primarily in the Mahgreb, they later saw service in all the wars in which France was involved. The Armée d'Afrique also included the colonial strike force, the French Foreign Legion (*Légion Etrangère*) and other units made up of penal conscripts from the French Army.

At the beginning of World War II the Armée d'Afrique had over 70 regiments serving on all fronts, but after the Fall of France in 1940 it was reduced to 120,000 men by the Vichy government at the Germans' behest. However, following the invasion of Tunisia by the Allies in 1943, a resurrected Armée d'Afrique then became the basis of all the Free French Forces that were not in the UK with de Gaulle. They were commanded by the dynamic Général Jean de Lattre de Tassigny and became Armée B,

A French Expeditionary Corps (*Corps Expéditionaire Français en Italie*, CEFI) composed of 112,000 soldiers, (60% mainly Moroccan Maghrebis and 40% French) and commanded by Gén Alphonse Juin was assigned to the US Fifth Army and sent to Italy in September 1943, where it won high praise from the Americans for its professionalism and tenacity.

By the time Operation Dragoon began, the Armée d'Afrique had seven divisions with over 250,000 men, and would play a key role in the liberation of most of southern France within a month including the port facilities of Marseilles and Toulon which were taken by the French. Composed of 82% experienced soldiers from units of the Armée d'Afrique (50% North Africans and 32% Pied-Noirs, 10% of Black Africans, and 8% urban French). In the divisions, the percentage of Maghrebi soldiers ranged from 27% in 1DB (armor) to 56% in 2DIM (motorized infantry). By weapon type, this percentage was about 70% in the skirmisher regiments, 40% in the engineers, and 30% in the artillery.

As more French fighters flocked to de Lattre, his army swelled to almost 400,000 and on September 25 these mixed units of French Armée B, French Forces of the Interior (FFI), the Resistance, and other volunteers were renamed French First Army. Fighting its way up the Rhône valley and through the Vosges Mountains, it would go on to liberate Strasbourg on November 23, break through the Siegfried Line, cross the Rhine and the Danube, and end the war in Austria.

A L'ARMEE NOIRE
"Passant,
ils sont tombés
fraternellement unis
pour que tu restes Français.
Léopold Sedar Senghor

Postwar the Armée d'Afrique returned to the Mahgreb and the units to their respective countries, although some were used in Indochina in 1946–1954. Today, apart from the Foreign Legion and one mechanized regiment of Spahis, all units of the Armée d'Afrique were disbanded or lost their former identity between 1960 and 1965 and joined the armies of their native countries once they became independent from France. In 1998 one mechanized regiment of chasseurs (*1er Regiment de Chasseurs d'Afrique*) was re-established to preserve the traditions of this famous unit. Other units, of Tirailleurs and artillery (*68e Régiment d'Artillerie d'Afrique*), have also been reestablished. The Foreign Legion remains one of France's elite forces, with over 9,000 men in 11 units, including six operational regiments.

Below and Opposite, Below:
Sculptor Yvon Guidez created this striking bronze in 1995. Five figures represent soldiers of the Armée d'Afrique with a white officer holding the French flag. The inscription— "Passers-by, they fell fraternally united so that you remain French"—is signed by Leopold Sedar Senghor (1906–2001), Senegalese politician and writer, and former President of the Republic of Senegal.

Much French Army equipment was American, and as the French First Army fought alongside the US Seventh, the same problems discussed on pp. 24–25 applied to each army. Toward the end of the year and into 1945, fighting in the Vosges Mountains saw heavy rain and snowfall. While each serviceman had been issued with two pairs of service shoes, there were insufficient galoshes The injury figures were high. During one week in October, there were 110 cases of trench-foot. In November it was cold injury: 662 cases one week in November, 907 cases the next. The French situation was made more difficult as the size of its army grew—not from trained replacements but by osmosis as huge numbers of FFI troops were subsumed into the French Army.

1 It wasn't just Frenchmen who flocked to the cause. These are the "Merlinettes," radio operators for Armée B HQ.

2, 3, and 6 The US provided most of the French forces' equipment: Dodge weapons carriers (**2**), M4A4 Shermans—this one is named Valmy (**3**)—M10 TDs (these are of 2/7RCA).

4 A nurse checking her Dodge ambulance's engine.

5 Significant numbers of French colonial troops fought in First Army. These are Algerians.

JEAN DE LATTRE DE TASSIGNY
MARECHAL DE FRANCE
1889 1952

GÉNÉRAL JEAN DE LATTRE DE TASSIGNY
(February 2, 1889–January 11, 1952)

Handsome and flamboyant, coming from an aristocratic family, Jean de Lattre de Tassigny attended French Naval School in 1908–1911 then transferred to the cavalry at Saumur. By 1912 he was a second lieutenant in the 12th Dragoons and when World War I broke out he saw action immediately, was wounded twice, and was awarded the Legion d'Honneur. In 1915 he was promoted to captain and transferred to the 93rd Infantry Division, fighting at Verdun for 16 months, being wounded five times and receiving eight citations and a Military Cross. He was then assigned to General Staff Headquarters of 21st Infantry Division. 1919 saw him transferred to the 49th Infantry Regiment at Bayonne. His next posting, 1921–1926, was Morocco, where he was again wounded, received three citations and was promoted to major. He then returned to the General Staff Headquarters.

On March 22, 1939, he became the youngest general in the French Army when he was promoted brigadier general, becoming Chief of Staff of the Fifth Army in September that same year. In January the following year he was given command of the 14th Infantry Division which fought against the Germans with distinction at Rethel, Champagne-Ardenne, and Mourmelon, and conducted successful rearguard actions on the Marne, Yvonne, Loire, and Nevers. After the armistice he remained in the now Vichy army. And concentrated on teaching and training his troops. Following the November 8, 1942, Allied landings in French North Africa, the Vichy forces were disbanded by the Nazis and Vichy was taken over by the Nazis. De Lattre, then in Montpellier, fought back and was imprisoned for a while in Riom Prison. In September 1943 he escaped to London to join de Gaulle, who sent de Lattre to Algiers to organize the Free French forces there. Promoted in

December 1943 by de Gaulle to the highest active military rank of général d'armée, he assumed command of the freshly formed Armée B, consisting mainly of the French Army of Africa along with other Free French troops and volunteers and began shaping it into a cohesive fighting force. By the time Operation Dragoon began, de Lattre had seven divisions—over 250,000 men—which combined with three US divisions and some special and airborne forces, made up the US Seventh Army. Within a month de Lattre had taken Marseilles and Toulon, the port facilities of which were reopened by September 20. As more French fighters flocked to de Lattre, his army swelled to almost 400,000 and on September 25 these mixed units of French Armée B, French Forces of the Interior, the Resistance, and other volunteers was renamed French First Army. Fighting its way up the Rhône valley and through the Vosges Mountains, it would go on to liberate Strasbourg on November 23, break through the Siegfried Line, cross the Rhine and the Danube, and end the war in Austria. During that time de Lattre had the honor of being the only French general to command US troops, when various American units were assigned to French First Army as reinforcements.

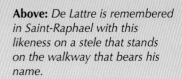

After the war, de Lattre became Inspector-General of the French Army 1945–1947. In 1950–1951 he commanded the French troops in French Indochina, inflicting various defeats on the Viet Minh and earning respect from his adversary Gen Giap. Tragically, however, he lost his only son, Lt Bernard de Lattre de Tassigny, who was killed at the battle of Nam Dinh, in late May 1951. Later that year illness forced his return to France, where on January 11, 1952, he died from cancer.

He was posthumously promoted to Maréchal (Marshal) de France and given a state funeral. Many memorials were erected in his memory and squares, boulevards, and streets all over France bear his name.

Above: *De Lattre is remembered in Saint-Raphael with this likeness on a stele that stands on the walkway that bears his name.*

Below Left: *De Lattre signing the German surrender documents in 1945 in the name of France. The German signatories were Keitel, Luftwaffe General Stumpf, and Admiral Freudenburg; the Allies had Zukhov and Tedder with Spaatz (left) and de Lattre as witnesses.*

Below: *De Lattre in 1946.*

This page: *The battery at Mauvanne had four 15cm TbKC/36 guns to protect Hyères Bay and, thereby, access to the city of Toulon. As was the case all along the Atlantic and Mediterranean coasts, in 1943 the Germans began emplacing the batteries and Mauvanne received M272 gun emplacements and a command bunker. Well-sited on a hill, the unit defenses commanded good fields of fire. Manned by 3./MAA 627, the battery was attacked and taken by commandos during the night of August 14/15. A week later the battery was used against its former owners, bombarding the Golf Hotel strongpoint in La Grau.*

Opposite, Above: *8RCA M10 TD knocked out during the fighting around Hyères. The regiment had supported the 1DFL in Italy.*

Opposite, Center: *Badges of the constituent forces of 1DFL.*

Opposite, Below: *Memorial to 1DFL just outside Hyères near the Golf Hotel. The granite slab is inscribed:*

continued on p.95

Mauvanne Battery

"Passer-by, remember the 1ère Division Français Libre. After illustrious work in the Levant, in Africa from Bir Hakeim and El Alamein, Tunisia, then Italy, the volunteers of 1DFL disembarked at Cavalaire on August 16, 1944. During the victorious battle of Provence, assisted by the guns of the French and Allied navies, the division freed: Hyères, Carqueiranne, La Crau, Le Pradet, La Garden and reached the center of Toulon. The division liberated Lyon and Belfort, saved Strasbourg and finished its journey on the plains of the River Po after having taken the fortress of Author defended by feisty Germans. 1DFL is the only division to have fought throughout the war from 1940 to 1945." 1DFL became 1DMI in April 1944.

"A LA MEMOIRE DU CAPITAINE LAMY
ARRIVE LE PREMIER SUR LE MONT-FARON
LE 22 AOUT 1944
A LA TÊTE DE LA 3ᵉᵐᵉ COMPAGNIE
DU PREMIER BATAILLON DE CHOC
MORT AU CHAMP D'HONNEUR
LE 30 SEPTEMBRE 1944"

ICI EST TOMBÉ LE 23 AOUT
LE LIEUTENANT J.M.CH
DU 67ᵉᵐᵉ Rᵗ. A.A.
(3ᵉᵐᵉ DIVISION D'INFANTERIE ALG
EN ACCOMPLISSANT UNE MISSION
AUPRÈS DU 1ᵉʳ BATAILLON DE
DANS LA BATAILLE DE TOI

Toulon

The arrival of Armée B troops happened much more quickly than had originally been planned. As de Lattre was telling General Patch that he would secure Toulon and Marseille within two weeks, so the tools he needed were returning to French soil. The plan (see the map on p. 86) was for 1DFL to press on immediately to attack Toulon from Hyères. In his history of French First Army, de Lattre identified three phases of the battle for Toulon. First, the investment (August 20 and 21) saw Col Bonjour's unit (3RSAR and 7RTA) and Col de Linares' 3RTA advance around the top of Toulon to attack from the west as Brosset's 1DFL came in from the east through difficult fighting at Hyères, and Magnan's 9DIC had a similarly tough time slightly further north. Differences of opinion between de Larminat (who believed that the army should bypass Toulon and head for Avignon) and de Lattre led to the latter leaving command of the eastern thrust on August 21st. De Lattre took over this command in time for the second phase: the dismantling (August 22 and 23). This saw the French eastern attack force its way through fortified lines and high ground; from the west they made their way into the city, setting up positions to stop any retreating Germans. Finally, the third phase was the systematic reduction of the Germans' final positions: forts, blockhouses, and the Arsenal Maritime.

Left: Towering over Toulon, Mont Faron was taken by storm by 3/Bataillon de Choc on August 22. The preserved M4A1 HVSS has been named Provence and carries the blue crest edged with red around a cross of Lorraine—the insignia of 1DFL.

Below, Left to Right:
• Plaque remembering the leader of 3/I Bataillon de Choc, Capt Léon Lamy, who died a month later.

• Lt J.M. Chipier of 67e RAA from 3eme DIA who died on Mount Faron on August 23.

• The I Bataillon de Choc who stormed Mount Faron and helped liberate Toulon.

44

PIER

ENNE)

'APPUI

HOC

N

Ier BATAILLON DE CHOC

22 AOUT 1944
CHASSE DU
MONT FARON
L'OCCUPANT NAZI

21-24 AOUT 1944
PARTICIPE A LA
LIBERATION DE
TOULON

Above and Below: *View over Toulon. In the distance is Saint-Mandrier-sur-Mer. Once an island, during World War II 15 coastal defense batteries, Flak batteries, and four huge 340mm naval guns were installed on Cap Cépet (see p. 18) in two turrets. The Allies used naval forces to pound the turrets from August 19, including the battleship* Lorraine, *also armed with 340mm guns. USS* Nevada *and its 14-inch (356mm) guns eventually silenced it after 354 salvoes. The Germans on Saint-Mandrier-sur-Mer*

finally surrendered early on August 28 as French troops readied to cross the narrow causeway. The battle for Toulon left 2,700 Frenchmen dead or wounded; 17,000 Germans went into captivity. Note Fort Faron in the foreground of the 1944 photo.

Right: *The French Naval Base of Toulon seen from a bomber. In the center of the photograph warships occupy the docks today used by the* Charles de Gaulle *aircraft carrier seen below.*

ICI MÊME LE 23 AOUT 1944
DES ÉLEMENTS DU 3ᴱᴹᴱ SPAHIS ALGERIENS
DU BATAILLON DE CHOC DU 3ᴱᴹᴱ TIRAILLEURS
ALGERIENS ET DU 7ᴱᴹᴱ CHASSEURS D'AFRIQUE
ONT FAIT DE NOUVEAU FLOTTER
LE DRAPEAU FRANÇAIS SUR TOULON

Opposite, Above: *Men of Armée B march on Boulevard de Strasbourg, during the parade celebrating the city's recent liberation, August 28.*

Opposite, Below: *Soldiers in Toulon on August 26 during mopping up operations. Note the abandoned German vehicles requisitioned by French forces.*

Opposite, Inset: *Plaque remembering the units involved in raising the French flag over Toulon, August 23.*

Left: *The bodies of German soldiers killed during the fighting.*

Below: *This bus won't reach Toulon. While the French were taking the coastal areas, the US troops were advancing to and past the Blue Line: while Toulon surrendered, the retreating Germans were being hounded up the Rhône valley by Seventh Army.*

Marseille

The second French objective was Marseille, but rather than wait until Toulon had been taken, de Lattre attacked it at the same time. The battle raged from August 20 to the 28th, at the end of which France's second city was in the hands of Armée B. Casualties had been high in the campaign to date:

4,000 killed or wounded in nine days of fighting. But the enemy had suffered worse: two divisions destroyed; 37,000 prisoners—and more to come as those who got away were picked up on their way north. The soldiers who had achieved the victory were Général Monsabert's, "the tirailleurs of the 3e DIA, the Goumiers of the Moroccan Tabors, troopers, zouaves, and gunners of the 1st DB—followed by the motley, feverish, bewildering mass of the FFI ..."

Opposite, Above and Below:
Aerial views of Marseille, the lower area showing the docks being bombed. De Lattre describes the city thus: "not merely an immense city with wide suburbs. It had become a real camp, set, like Toulon, in a double defensive system ... there was nothing but blocks and casemates, articulated round the two principal redoubts—the port installations to the north, the hill of Notre-Dame de la Garde to the south ... All these positions, which possessed 150 to 200 guns of 75mm to 220mm, were occupied by a reinforced garrison."
Ralf Roletschek/WikiCommons
Roletschek.at ralf@roletschek.de

Above: *Even after much of the debris has been taken away, the damage left by the Germans in their attempts to make Marseille harbor unusable is obvious. The view looks over to Les Îles, with the Count of Monte Cristo's Château d'If at left.*

Above Right and Right: *The Musée des Civilisations de l'Europe et de la Méditerranée and the Villa Méditerranée (white building) now fill the gap between the Fort Saint Jean and Notre Dame de la Majeur.*

Above: M4A4 St Quentin *of 2e Cuirassiers, 1DB part of Sudré's CC1 which took part in the liberation of Marseille.*

Below: Jeanne d'Arc *also fought for 2e Cuirassiers, and can be seen today just down the hill from the Basilique Notre-Dame de la Garde. A storyboard explains: "The investment of the city was led by Col Chappuis at the head of the 7th RTA, supported by the tanks of 2RC. The assault on Basilique Notre-Dame de la Garde by the 1er and 2eme Companies, 7RTA and 2RC was one of the most dramatic episodes. The tank was hit and immobilized, three of its crew killed instantly. The vehicle was restored and inaugurated as a memorial on August 25, 1946."*

Opposite: *Scenes of Marseille during and after the fighting.*

1 and 2 *A strongpoint—pillbox, trenches, wire and 7.5cm PaK 97/38 antitank gun—at the intersection of Boulevard des Dames and Rue de la République, August 30.*

3 *PzKpfw II turret pillbox.*

4 *Men of the 7e RTA on the slopes heading up to Basilique Notre-Dame de la Garde. Note rifle grenade.*

5 and 6 *The destruction along Quai de la Joliette.*

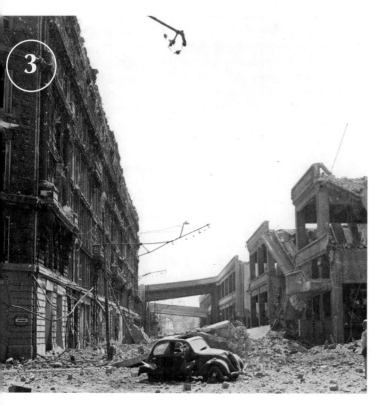

Above and Below: The Germans proved adept at harbor destruction: Naples, Cherbourg, Antwerp, and the Channel ports were all "decommissioned" thoroughly and efficiently. At Marseille only one of the port's piers proved serviceable. The harbor and port had been littered with mines, some with delayed action. There were no operational cranes and the enemy had learned from the speed with which the Allies had rehabilitated Naples.

Ships—65 ships, over 200,000 tons of them—had been sunk in the harbor, often with broken backs and positioned to cause the engineers as many problems as possible. By September 8 there were eight Liberty berths open and by the end of the month the port had dealt with 188 ships, 147,460 men, 113,500 long tons of cargo, 32,768 vehicles, and 10,000 of POL.

In spite of the Germans' best efforts, the Allies worked wonders. By September 1 DUKWs were able to unload Liberty ships and soon supplies were streaming through the port. As the 781st Tank Battalion's postwar history proudly proclaims, many men and munitions were sent "up from Marseille" and it proved more effective than Cherbourg. There was a debate between the US Army and Navy about whether Toulon or Marseille should be refurbished. The railroad system out of Marseille, which followed Seventh Army's route up the Rhône and could handle 350 boxcars a day, ensured Marseille won out. HQ and 2nd Battalion, 36th Engineer Combat Regiment and the 335th Engineer General Service Regiment moved in and went about the first job: clearing mines (over 2,000) and explosives (over 30 tons).

5 THE ADVANCE TO THE VOSGES

M4A1 crossing the Durance river at Mirabeau. A major tributary of the Rhône, which the Durance meets near Avignon, it can be fast-flowing and is a major obstacle.

The ease with which the landings were consolidated surprised everyone who was not privy to the ULTRA and intelligence reports. Expecting the backlash—a German counterattack spearheaded by 11. Panzer—in fact the intelligence told the real story: that the Germans had decided on August 17 that their strategy would be to retreat. With their forces in Normandy streaming back towards the Falaise Gap this is, perhaps, unsurprising. Had the Nineteenth Army held its ground, there's no doubt that it would have been even more cut up than it was as it retreated, ultimately ending up in a more defensive line in the Vosges Mountains. Essentially, this decision condemned the defenders of Toulon and Marseille—shortly to be threatened by the French Armée B—to holding out for as long as possible to drain Allied attempts to chase the rest of Nineteenth Army. It didn't work. As we have seen, the French catapulted out of the traps and, although it was a tough fight, took Toulon and Marseille within ten days, before heading north.

It is suggested that at this stage Patch and Truscott were too cautious. Had they advanced north faster and in more force they may have trapped German 198. Division and Kniess' LXXXV Corps south of the Durance. That may well have been the case, but it's easy to say in hindsight. The Allies' main problem was their lack of an armored spearhead. It was supposed to have been provided by the French Combat Command 1, led by Brig Gen Aime Sudre—and initially it was. Sudre's CC1 was tasked with advancing to Saint-Maximin, which it did, but then national priorities dug in and CC1 returned to de Lattre's command to assist in the taking of the ports. Much as Pershing had fought to ensure the American Expeditionary Force in WWI was not used in penny packets, so de Lattre fought to ensure his army fought as one. This usefully coincided with the overall need to take the ports and so Patch allowed CC1 to return to de Lattre.

Patch and Truscott had another plan, however: to combine the armor assets VI Corps had to hand to provide a fast-moving strike force. It was under the command of Brig Gen Frederick Butler: Task Force Butler.

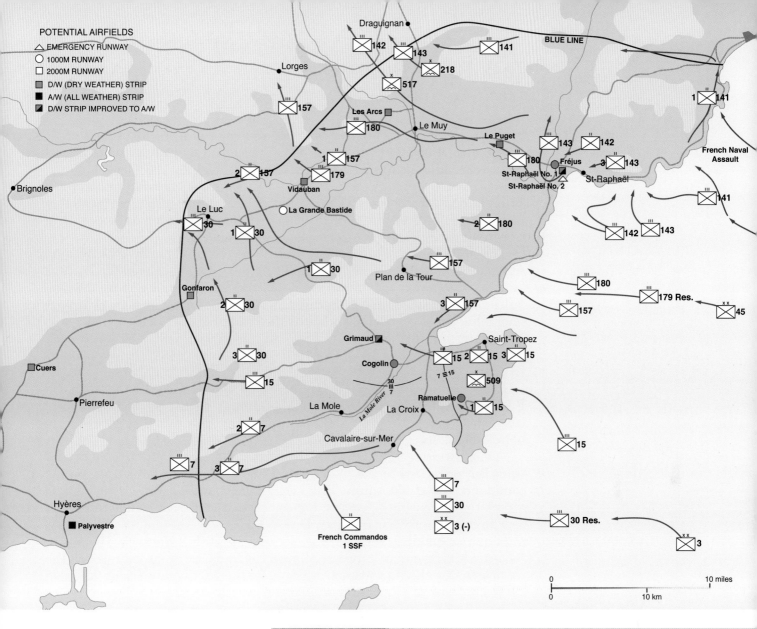

POTENTIAL AIRFIELDS
△ EMERGENCY RUNWAY
○ 1000M RUNWAY
□ 2000M RUNWAY
▨ D/W (DRY WEATHER) STRIP
■ A/W (ALL WEATHER) STRIP
◪ D/W STRIP IMPROVED TO A/W

Draguignan

BLUE LINE

142
143
218
517
141

Lorges

157

Les Arcs
180
Le Muy
Le Puget
143   142
180   Fréjus
3   143
St-Raphaël No. 1   St-Raphaël
St-Raphaël No. 2
French Naval Assault
1   141

1   157
179
Vidauban

2   157

Brignoles

La Grande Bastide

Le Luc
30
1   30

1   30

Plan de la Tour

2   180

142   143

180

157

179 Res.

45

Gonfaron

2   30

3   157

3   30

Saint-Tropez
15 2   15   3   15
509
7   15

15
Grimaud
Cogolin
30
7
Ramatuelle
1   15

Cuers

Pierrefeu

2   7

La Mole   La Croix
La Môle River

Cavalaire-sur-Mer

15

Hyères
Palyvestre

3   7
7

French Commandos
1 SSF

7

30

3 (-)

30 Res.

3

0 _____ 10 miles
0 _____ 10 km

Below and Right: *La Garde-Freinet in the hills above Saint-Tropez and Sainte-Maxime has changed little in the intervening years. The locals knew then what they expected: Berlin that way!*

111

Task Force Butler

TASK FORCE BUTLER UNITS

Brigadier General William B. Butler

117th Cavalry Reconnaissance Squadron
59th Armored Field Artillery Battalion
753rd Tank Battalion (less 1 x medium and 1 x light companies)
2nd Battalion, 143rd Infantry Regiment (27 rifle squads)
Company C, 636th Tank Destroyer Battalion
Company C, 111th Medical Battalion
Detachment, Company D, 111th Medical Battalion
3426th QM Truck Company
Detachment, 87th Ordnance Company
Detachment, VI Corps MPs

TASK FORCE BUTLER VEHICLES AND MAIN ARMAMENT

M8 Greyhound armored cars (37mm)	40
M3/M5 light tanks (37mm)	17
M4 Shermans (75mm and 76mm)	34
M4 Shermans (105mm)	2
M10 Tank Destroyers (3 inch)	12
M7 Priest SP artillery (105mm howitzers)	18
M8 75mm HMCs (75mm)	6
Jeeps	135
M3 Halftracks	26

From the start, Truscott had wanted an armored force to be part of VI Corps, but US armored divisions were spread thinly in August 1944, and none was available. French CC1 was available for a few days after landing, but not for long enough. So, on August 1, two weeks before the landings, Truscott instructed his staff to organize a suitable unit from available forces—mainly from the 36th Division. It would be commanded by Brig Gen William B. Butler, VI Corps deputy commander.

The units that would form TF Butler concentrated north of Le Muy on August 17, and were let off the leash the next day. It existed for 14 days and in that period "advanced over 235 miles, liberated approx 6,645sq miles of Southern France, captured more than 3,500 German prisoners (including three generals), and destroyed hundreds of German vehicles."

Advancing north and west, TF Butler advanced nearly 50 miles each day on August 18 (to Riez), the 19th (to Sisteron), the 20th (Aspres-sur-Beuch).

Ready to advance toward Grenoble, on the evening of the 20th TF Butler was ordered west toward Montélimar to cut off the retreat of German Nineteenth Army. 36th Infantry Division was also en route to help the task force.

Leaving protection to guard against an attack from Grenoble and Gap, Butler moved to the high ground above Montélimar, setting up his command post at Marsanne. From the high ground TF Butler was able to attack the retreating Germans, but not block the retreat completely.

The arrival of 36th Infantry Division HQ saw the end of TF Butler, although a smaller version was set up as 36th Infantry's Divisional Reserve, seeing action between August 25–29 as it attempted to block the roads north to the retreating Germans. Its final act before deactivation on August 30 was to attack and take Loriol-sur-Drôme.

Above: *753rd Tank Battalion M4A1 KO'd during the battle of Montélimar in fighting with 11. Panzer Div near Grane August 28.*

Below: *Patrol of 117th Cavalry Recon Squadron fords the River Verdon near Riez.*

US 3rd Infantry Division

The 3rd Infantry Division's three regiments (7th, 15th, and 30th) landed on Alpha beaches Red and Blue and quickly moved off the beach into the Saint-Tropez peninsula. Clearing the area—Saint-Tropez had been taken by the Resistance and elements of 509th PIB—the 15th and 30th Regiments headed along the road to Aix while 7th took the southerly route toward Toulon. The units on the northern route moved smoothly until they reached Brignoles, where heavy resistance by II/ Infanterie-Regiment 757 of German 338. Infantry Division held up the advance for a day until a three-pronged attack saw the town taken by 11:00 on the 19th.

Joined by the 7th Regiment (once its positions had been taken over by French units), the division advanced quickly on Aix, accelerating the German retreat and stopping them from setting up a defensive line there.

Advancing up the Rhône valley, the 3rd Division pressurized the retreating Germans, but logistics problems, mines, booby traps, and other delays meant that they only clashed occasionally with the rearguard until the 28th when they fought running battles all day, finally reaching Montélimar and clearing it by the morning of the 29th.

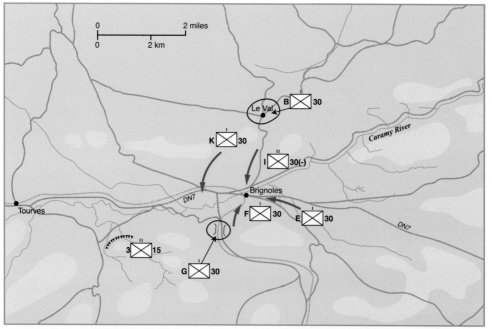

Opposite, Above and Center: *3rd Infantry Division troops and a Sherman of French CC1 enter Flassans-sur-Issole, a pretty Provençal town on the road to Brignoles.*

Opposite, Below: *M4 of 756th Tank Battalion KO'd outside Flassans. It was hit twice: once below the driver's hatch and the second in the transmission plate.*

Above: *3rd Division's shoulder patch.*

Above Left: *The battle of Brignoles saw 30th Infantry supported by French CC1 take the town.*

Left and Below: *2/15th Infantry Regiment heading toward Brignoles. The 15th Division—the "Rock of the Marne"—gained its nickname in WWI and had a long WWII, sailing to North Africa for Operation Torch in October 1942 and fighting in Sicily and Italy. It would lose 1,633 men killed during the war and have 16 Medal of Honor winners, including Audie Murphy (p. 178); it also numbered Dwight Eisenhower among its alumni. He was a lieutenant in the regiment in 1940.*

Above and Right: *Brignoles has fallen and Allied armor heads through on the Aix road. The M7 howitzer motor carriage boasted a 105mm and a tall MG position which reminded the British of a pulpit—accounting for their name for it: the Priest.*

Below and Below Right: *Men of F/30th Infantry Regiment sitting in front of the Brignoles WWI war memorial. Note the NSKK sign in the background—the National Socialist Motor Corps which had a French section.*

Above: *Provence is a hot place in August—particularly for footsloggers.*

Left and Far Left *The speed of the advance precluded stringing wire, so the Signal Corps refurbished 1,715 miles of the existing French wire—as here on the road from Brignoles to Aix. The official history points out the good radio communications but the shortage of large scale tactical maps caused by the speed of the advance. TF Butler was forced to use tourist guide maps and 1:50,000 maps weren't available till mid-September.*

Top Left: *Wounded German being carried to a first aid station by his comrades. They were captured on the outskirts of Brignoles by troops of the 2/15 Infantry Regiment.*

Top Right: *Walking over Hitler—a good image for the cameraman.*

Above: *The fleeing German Nineteenth Army made a good target for air attack. Here, on the way to Tourves on August 22, the German vehicles have been cleared to the side of the road.*

Right: *The Resistance search out collaborators in Aix. Summary justice was often the result.*

This page: *Blaskowitz planned the retreat of Army Group G carefully, selecting three defensive lines to allow the units in southwest, southern, and southeast France to effect a retreat behind the screen. The units in the northern southwest were to move east and meet up with the main body around Lyon; those in the extreme south were to meet Blaskowitz's army around Avignon. ULTRA intercepts on August 17 and 18 ensured Patch knew what was happening, but he was more concerned with protecting French First Army's northern flank and didn't have the trucks and the gasoline to attack toward Avignon where 11. Panzer, 198. and 338. Infantry Divisions were crossing the Rhône on small ferries. The Allied push west was limited to Aix which was taken by August 22 as the storyboard remembers (**Below**). These photos show US armor in the form of an M8 HMC (**Above Left**) and an M8 armored car with an M20 utility car behind (**Below Left**). The fountain is the famous 1860 Fontaine de la Rotonde in Aix.*

119

45th Infantry Division

The Thunderbirds were part of the Oklahoma National guard, and had fought in Sicily, at Salerno and elsewhere in Italy before taking part in Operation Dragoon. Originally commanded by Troy Middleton, arthritis forced a change and Maj Gen William Eagles took over, leading the division at Anzio. Landing over the Delta sector beaches, the 45th's three regiments—the 157th, 159th, and 180th—were tasked with clearing Sainte-Maxime, taking the high ground overlooking the Argens Valley from the south, and linking up with the paratroopers of Rugby Force and the 36th Division, who landed to their north around Saint-Raphaël. This the 45th did, reaching the Blue Line by August 16. VI Corps commander Lucien Truscott next pushed west with 3rd and 45th infantry divisions, and the 45th liberated Le Luc, Barjols (on the 19th), Mirabeau, Pertuis (the 20th), and Apt (the 22nd). Then pushed towards Grenoble, elements of the division took part in the battle of Montélimar.

Above and Right: After moving up to help the paratroopers in Le Muy, the 45th headed west. Vidauban was liberated by 157th Infantry on the 17th. The retreating Germans left behind many of their weapons including this 2cm antiaircraft gun in place de la Montagne, very little changed today (other than the removal of the weapon).

Above: *Sgt Theodore Valard of B Coy, 191st Tank Battalion commanded this tank knocked out at point-blank range by an 88 on August 19, south of Rians. The 191st was attached to 45th Division for much of the campaign.*

Left: *Men of the 45th pause in Pertuis. The town fell on the August 20.*

Below: *45th infantrymen hitch a lift on a 645th TD Bn M10 north of Salernes, August 18.*

Right and Below Right: *The Durance is a significant obstacle to any force heading north from the Mediterranean to the Alps or Aix-en-Provence and the Rhône valley. At the Defile de Mirabeau there have been a number of bridges. This postcard shows the two old bridges, that to the left was built in 1847 to replace the first, 1835, bridge which lasted but eight years before it was swept away in a flood. The one to the right was built in 1934 and survived until 1944. There were a number of attempts to bomb it but it finally succumbed to 20kg of plastic explosives fired by the Resistance around 21:30 on August 17. The Americans were able to erect a footbridge (**Below Right**), but had to build a pontoon bridge (**opposite**).*

Below: *The bridge was rebuilt after the war until replaced by the existing structure in 1989. Véronique Pagnier/WikiCommons (CC BY-SA 3.0)*

Opposite, Above: *A 645th TD Battalion M10 crosses the Durance, benefitting from the good weather and low water.*

Opposite, Center and Below: *Class 40 bridge built by 120th Engineer Battalion.*

MIRABEAU (Vaucluse) _ Le Pont

36th Infantry Division

Landing around Saint-Raphaël, the role of the Texans—nicknamed thus because they were part of the Texas National Guard—in the early part of the pursuit of the retreating Germans was to hold the eastern flank of the invasion—especially against a possible counterattack from Italy over the Alpine passes. As soon as the 1st SSF and 1st AATF were able to take over this mission, the 36th was set up to advance to Grenoble, but it was ordered to join Task Force Butler around Montélimar to catch Army Group G, with a regiment of the 45th attached. Trouble was that logistically Seventh Army was stuttering. From the start it had been short of trucks and gas, and even capturing German fuel dumps didn't help sufficiently. When Truscott's orders reached 36th Division's CG, Major General John E. Dahlquist, most of the division's trucks were either with TF Butler or being used for resupply and were not in place to transport troops. Truscott and Dahlquist also had their problems, the latter not having been part of Truscott's Italian team, and the two hadn't got to know each other's styles.

In the forthcoming battle of Montélimar, VI Corps let slip an opportunity to crush the retreating German Army Group G. The prime reason for this was logistics—fuel supplies and ammunition shortages—but analysis of the battle shows hesitancy on the part of the higher command, Patch and Truscott, to concentrate their forces. Dahlquist, their man on the ground, was similarly unsure and tentative. Concern about German threats from Gap and Grenoble also helped hold back men who could otherwise have been tightening the noose around the retreating Germans.

Right: *A map of the 36th Division's experiences from its arrival in France.*

Below: *36th Infantry march through Draguignan toward Grenoble. Today Draguignan is the site of the Rhône American Cemetery and Memorial.*

Opposite, Above: *The advance from the Blue Line. Initially speedy, the advance slowed as fuel became scarce. The army needed 100,000 gallons a day and only 11,000 was coming over the beaches.*

Opposite, Below: *The first American troops to reach Grenoble, August 28.*

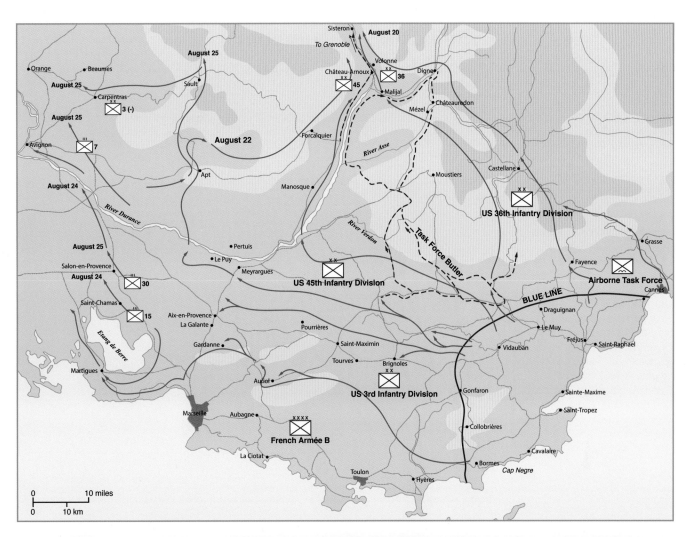

1 *As Army Group G streamed up both sides of the Rhône—IV Luftwaffe Corps on the west and LXXXV Corps on the east—on August 21 Task Force Butler moved into position from the direction of Grenoble and took the high ground around Hill 300 along the N7 highway south of La Coucourde. Butler set up his HQ in Marsanne (memorial plaque* **inset opposite***). Elements of 36th Infantry Division—141st Infantry Regiment—linked up with the task force. However, worried about sightings of 11. Panzer south of the Durance—it's a German ruse to make US forces think a counterattack is imminent; it works—Truscott waits until 23:00 before ordering Dahlquist's 36th Division to move west in force. Northeast of Montélimar there's fighting at Sauzet and the Germans advanced along the Roubion taking Puy-Saint-Martin. They were pushed back by the last elements of Task Force Butler coming from the Grenoble area.*

2 *During August 22 and 23 the rest of 36th Division arrived and took up a blocking position along the River Roubion from Puy-Saint-Martin toward Montélimar. Battalions of VI Corps artillery—two of 155mms—arrived to give Dahlquist's forces some teeth. The Germans—in the form of Kampfgruppe Hax and elements of 198. Infantry Division—attacked along this line on August 25–26.*

3 *Some 500 miles from Montélimar, around Chambois and Mont-Ormel, at the end of August, Army Group B was being crushed in killing fields patrolled by Allied fighter-bombers. On the banks of the Rhône similar scenes were being enacted. Just outside Montélimar on August 30, a 3rd Division M10 tank destroyer passes through a scene of devastation.*

4 *More destruction. Here, a 105mm Flak 38/39 gun—note the size of the round on ground beside the gun.*

5 *M10 of 601st TD Bn assigned to 3rd Division outside Le Colombier south of Montélimar.*

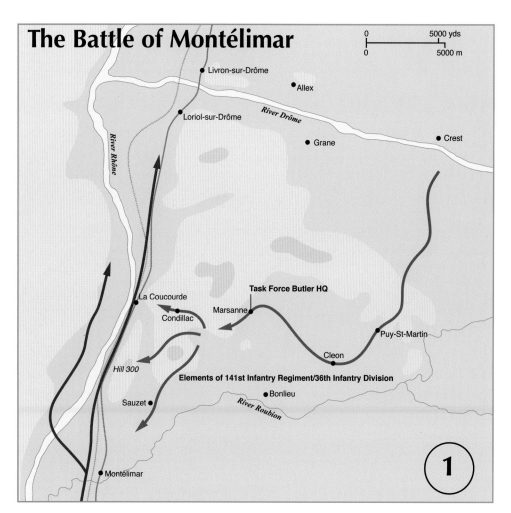

The Battle of Montélimar

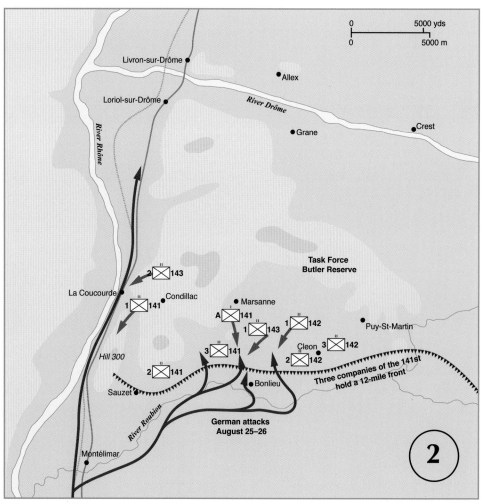

ICI
A MARSANNE DU 21 AU 29 AOUT 1944
LA TASK FORCE BUTLER
ET
LA 36 eme DIVISION TEXAS
ONT ETABLI LEUR QUARTIER GENERAL
LORS DE LA BATAILLE DE MONTELIMAR
MARSANNE LE 23-08-1996

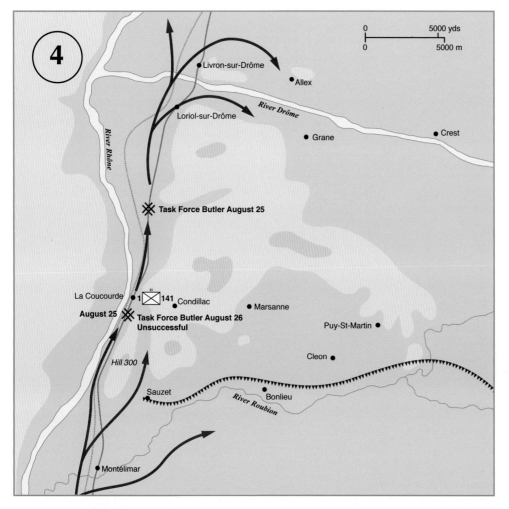

1 Maj Fezell, 3rd Infantry Division Signal Officer, looks over maps with his staff in Valréas, August 28. Note the shoulder patches for 3rd Infantry and VI Corps) and the three US Signal Corps lapel pins. Note also the attendant FFI men: the contribution of the French Maquis was significant.

2 The corridor of death on August 28. This M8 is leaving Allan and traveling up N7.

3 German snipers captured in Montélimar, August 29.

4 August 25–27 were the critical days of the battle. The Germans had found a copy of Dahlquist's plan of action on the evening of the 24th and von Wietersheim devised a complicated plan that would—he hoped—end with the US forces encircled. In the north the attack pushed aside 117th Cavalry Recon Squadron and the Germans took Grane and Crest. Elsewhere, they ran into trouble, and as the fighting intensified, TF Butler was able to get troops across the N7 just north of Coucourde. This roadblock was destroyed by an ad hoc unit led by von Wietersheim that knocked out three tanks, six TDs and retook Hill 300. On the 26th US forces tried to cut the N7 corridor from the Condillac Pass and, although managing to do so temporarily, were repulsed. August 27 saw more reinforcements (157th Infantry) but 3rd Division coming up from the south were finding it hard going, hampered by transport issues, booby traps, and mines.

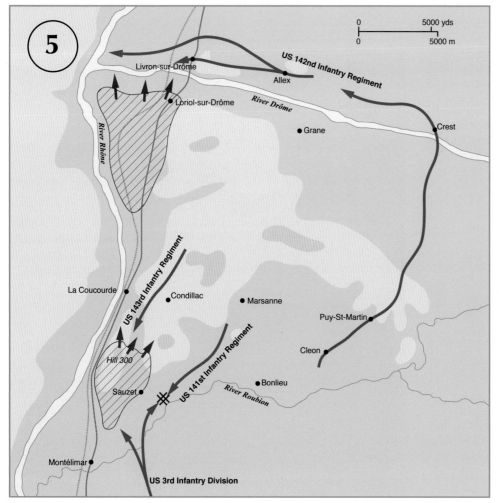

5 August 29–31 saw the final act in the battle as the Germans kept the road open for long enough for the bulk of their forces to get clear, but with mounting losses. Finally, with Montélimar cleared by the 3rd Division, on August 29 the German rearguard formed into three columns and headed over the Drôme. US 142nd Infantry was able to meet two of these columns and take prisoners, but the third column got away.

Scenes of devastation along the N7 from Montélimar. Note the civilian buses. The German Army was poorly motorized and depended greatly on horse-drawn vehicles—and they don't move very quickly when you're trying to outpace the US Army. Luckily for the Germans, they did not have to face the same intensity of air attack that they did in Normandy, and the fuel supply problems held the motorized Americans back or the scale of the German defeat might have been bigger. Today, the west bank houses France's Cruas Nuclear Power Station whose cooling towers are seen in the then and now pairing opposite.

The "butcher's bill" (as identified in the official history) belies the duration of the battle and intensity of the fighting. On the American side, the total casualty figure was 1,575—187 dead, 1,023 wounded, and 365 missing. The Germans lost considerably more—870 dead, 2,080 wounded, 8,000 captured or missing—but the bulk of their forces had got away, including 11. Panzer Division whose 750 casualties reduced it to 12,500 men. 11. Panzer also brought back 39 of 42 artillery pieces, 30 tanks (of 40 or so) and 75 percent of its other vehicles.

But from where Patch and the Allied High Command were sitting, the overall picture was rosy. With Toulon and Marseille in Allied hands, supply problems would improve. The Allies had cleared southern France from the Gironde to the Italian border ridiculously quickly. The hard fighting was about to begin.

Nineteenth Army had a number of railway gun batteries available at the start of Operation Dragoon. Most were lost in the fighting around Montélimar.

Above: The largest railway gun available for the defense of southern France were the two 38cm K.(E) "Siegfried" guns of Railway Battery 698. They were originally designed for use in the German pocket battleships, but were incorporated as railway guns. This one was named Gneisenau, the other Scharnhorst.

Below Right Bruno, a 27.4cm K.(E) 592 (f) of Railway Battery 692 captured near Le Logis Neuf.

The battle between the Roubion and the Drôme may have ended, but the pursuit didn't. The Germans were still severely pressured: Army Group G was still retreating: LXIV Corps heading east from the Atlantic coast was still to get to safety. Seventh Army was still hot on their heels. Additionally, with Toulon and Marseille taken, de Lattre's forces were heading north. Only two weeks after the landings on the Riviera, Patch's command closed on Lyon where the "Champagne Campaign" would finish. The Sixth Army Group commanded by Devers was due to become operational under Eisenhower's overall control. 36th Infantry were tasked with advancing through Valence and Vienne to Lyon where an uprising had already begun; the 45th from Grenoble to Meximieux and Bourg. With the French moving up from the south there was another chance to trap the retreating Germans. South of Meximieux only one bridge was still intact and protected by the Maquis. The 45th's 179th Infantry Regiment, commanded by Col Henry Meyer, was sent to Meximieux as the division's other regiments, the 157th and 180th traveled north.

Above Right and Right: *Le Logis Neuf is north of La Coucourde on the N7.*

Below Left and Right: *On the banks of the Drôme, Loriol was taken by 142nd Infantry. Here, three tankers—presumably from 11. Panzer—sit on the steps of Loriol's war memorial.*

Opposite: *After Lyon, French First Army contributed materially to the advance.*

Toward Lyon

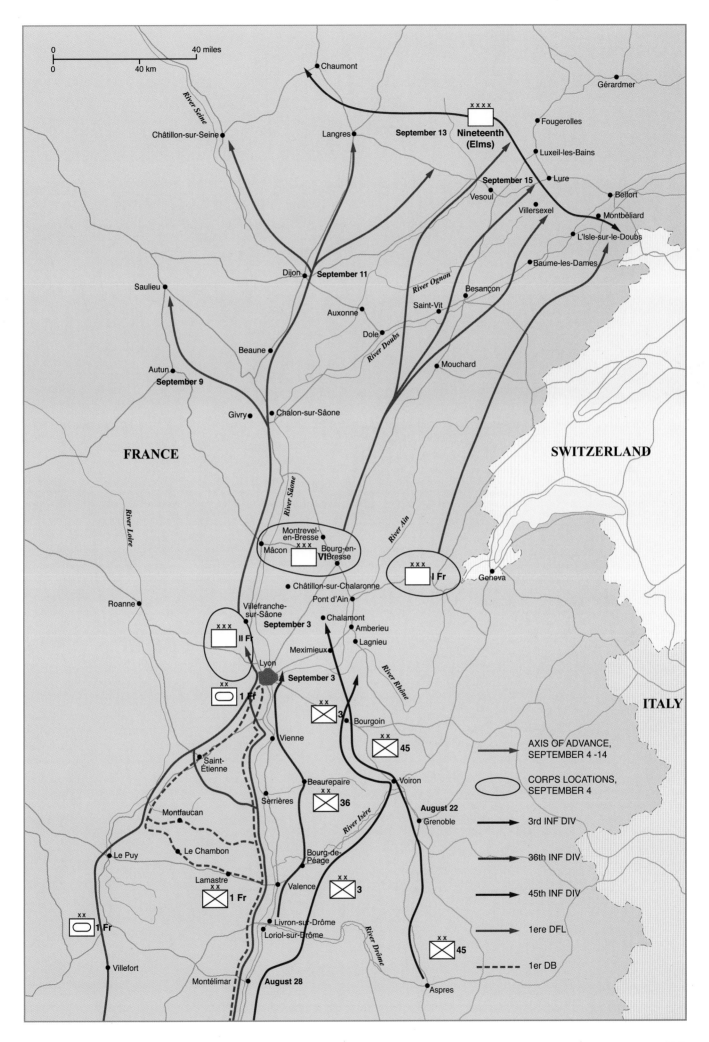

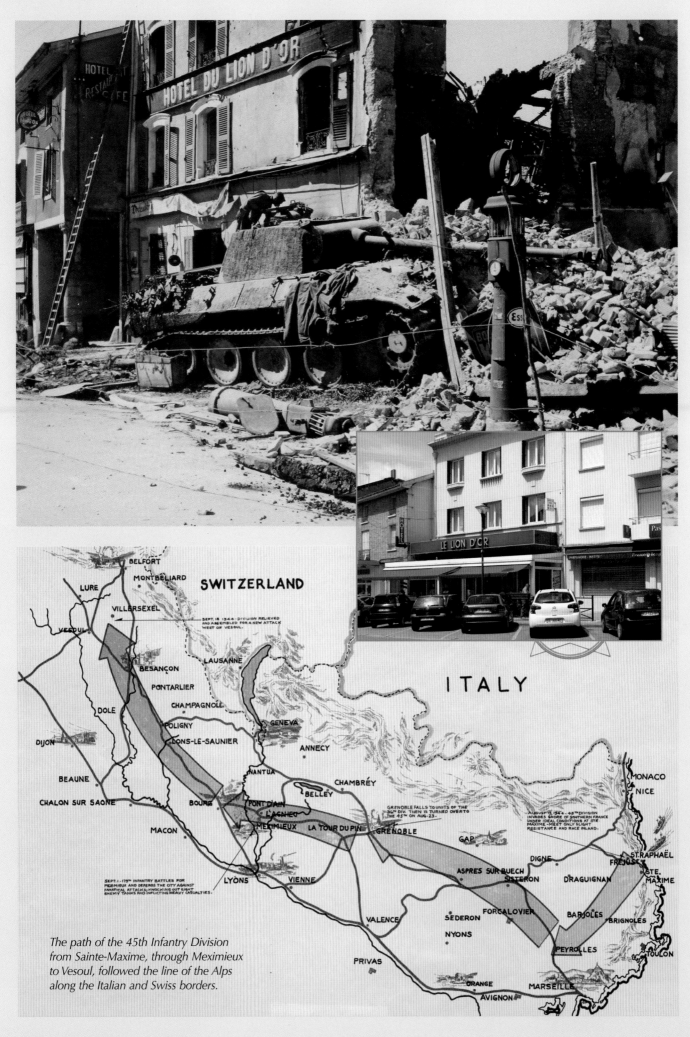

The path of the 45th Infantry Division from Sainte-Maxime, through Meximieux to Vesoul, followed the line of the Alps along the Italian and Swiss borders.

THE BATTLE OF MEXIMIEUX

The 45th Infantry Division weren't novices. They had seen action in Italy and had taken part in the lightning campaign up from the Riviera— but even the veterans must have paled when the 11. Panzer Division Kampfgruppe attacked the 179th Infantry Regiment. The 179th's executive officer, Col Preston J. C. Murphy, was ensconced in the local seminary with F Company five miles forward towards Lyon, and 1st Battalion, led by a future NATO and West Point commander, Lt Col Michael Davison, deployed around the station. FFI troops, led by Capt Clin, bolstered the numbers in the seminary. Made up of elements of Panzer-Regiments 15 and 209, and Panzergrenadier-Regiment 111, the German counterattack started on August 31. Its aim was to hold up the advancing Americans so that the main body of Army Group G could retreat in safety, and its attack started well. F Co was routed with 300 prisoners. But from the tower of the seminary, US artillery observers rained fire down on the Germans from 189th Field Artillery Battalion. Ammo ran so low that the battery ammunition train had to run the gauntlet back to get more. In the town itself, Murphy's men held out at the seminary, even after the nearby château was captured. Davison had two tank destroyers positioned in the town center and they were used to effect when six German tanks, each carrying infantry, moved into town. The M10s and bazooka teams did a brilliant job: amazingly, even a mortar of D Co was credited with a Panther kill when a direct hit on top of the turret set off the internal ammunition. When the mauled Kampfgruppe retreated, it left behind at least 15 armored vehicles.

Opposite, Above and Inset: *One of the Panthers 11. Panzer lost in street fighting in Meximieux. Today, the rebuilt Lion d'Or lacks its nearby petrol pump but at least there's room on the terrace.*

Below: *Three photos showing the aftermath of the battle: two more KO'd Panthers (on La Plaine and in Place de la Poste—now Place Lt Giraud) and a PzKpfw III on La Plaine. These photos are used with the permission of www.45thdivision.org. They were taken by Gerald Hall, a mechanic in the 157th Infantry Regiment, after the battle. Figures on the German losses vary but could be as high as 10 Panthers, 1 Panzer III, 2 Hummel, 1 Italian tank, 1 captured Greyhound, 3 SdKfz251s and 10 trucks and light vehicles. They had 85 dead and 41 captured. US losses amounted to 3 dead, 27 wounded, and 185 missing or captured, with 2 TDs destroyed along with 2 armored cars, and 23 other vehicles.*

MEDAL OF HONOR CITATION DANIEL W. LEE

1Lt. (then 2Lt.) Daniel W. Lee was leader of Headquarters Platoon, Troop A, 117th Cavalry Reconnaissance Squadron, Mechanized, at Montrevel, France, on September 2, 1944, when the Germans mounted a strong counterattack, isolating the town and engaging its outnumbered defenders in a pitched battle. After the fight had raged for hours and our forces had withstood heavy shelling and armor-supported infantry attacks, 2d Lt. Lee organized a patrol to knock out mortars which were inflicting heavy casualties on the beleaguered reconnaissance troops. He led the small group to the edge of the town, sweeping enemy riflemen out of position on a ridge from which he observed 7 Germans manning 2 large mortars near an armored half-track about 100 yards down the reverse slope. Armed with a rifle and grenades, he left his men on the high ground and crawled to within 30 yards of the mortars, where the enemy discovered him and unleashed machine-pistol fire which shattered his right thigh. Scorning retreat, bleeding and suffering intense pain, he dragged himself relentlessly forward. He killed 5 of the enemy with rifle fire and the others fled before he reached their position. Fired on by an armored car, he took cover behind the German half-track and there found a Panzerfaust with which to neutralize this threat. Despite his wounds, he inched his way toward the car through withering machine-gun fire, maneuvering into range, and blasted the vehicle with a round from the rocket launcher, forcing it to withdraw. Having cleared the slope of hostile troops, he struggle back to his men, where he collapsed from pain and loss of blood. 2d Lt. Lee's outstanding gallantry, willing risk of life, and extreme tenacity of purpose in coming to grips with the enemy, although suffering from grievous wounds, set an example of bravery and devotion to duty in keeping with the highest traditions of the military service.

Opposite, Above: *Valence welcomes American troops.*

Opposite, Below Right and Left: *Obelisk remembering the fiftieth anniversary of the arrival of American troops—117th Cavalry Recon—in Montrevel-en-Bresse. It was here that elements of the 117th suffered the fate of so many small, lightly armed recon assets when they outpace their protective artillery and air cover. On September 3 two troops took Montrevel—a small town some way ahead of the US 45th Infantry Division and on 11. Panzer's supply route. The inevitable happened and 11. Panzer sent a Kampfgruppe to see 117th Cavalry off. The two troops fought like tigers, but surrounded by a larger force, with too many wounded to attempt a breakout, and ammunition almost spent, 126 men of 117th Cavalry had to surrender. During the action, 2Lt Daniel W. Lee's bravery led to the award of the Congressional Medal of Honor.* Chabe01

Above: *Place Bellecour in Lyon, September 3. The French were given the honor of liberating Lyon.* AFP/Getty Images

Left: *French women celebrating the liberation of Lyon, France's third city.* AFP/Getty Images

Following the battles at Meximieux and Montrevel, 11. Panzer had done what it had been asked to do: protected the flank of the retreating army. It was now scurrying past Maçon. This meant it was time for 11. Panzer to move off, and so they did. This left Bourg free for 45th Division (September 4), Maçon for 36th, and—as we have seen—Lyon for the French. Here, the 157th Infantry and the 191st Tank Battalion travel through Bourg to the delight of the crowds.

On September 4 Patch, de Lattre, and Truscott finalized orders for the forthcoming attack: French II Corps (under Gen de Monsabert) in the west would advance north from Lyon down the Saône toward Dijon. US VI Corps at Bourg would head toward Besançon; French I Corps (under Lt Gen Emile Bethouart) west of Geneva would hug the Swiss border heading for the Belfort Gap.

Above: *Chemilla, east of Chalon, is liberated. Note the canvas cover on the top of the M20 utility vehicle. This used the .50cal MG as a "ridge pole" and kept weather out of the fighting compartment.*

Below: *The pace of the advance shows itself in these weary soldiers and their canine companion on Saint-Germain-de-Bois station.*

Opposite: *As it left Lyon, Général Vigier's 1DB split into CC1 under Général Sudre and CC2 under Colonel Kienst. The defenders—IV Luftwaffe Field Corps—had destroyed the*

bridges meaning that Chalon-sur-Saône had to be attacked from the west bank, so it was 3RCA of CC1 that liberated the city in conjunction with the local FFI. It was a hard fight that took most of September 5, but by 16:30 the bells were ringing. Pont Saint-Laurent was rebuilt by Co D of 1303rd Engineer General Service Regiment.

On September 7, luck ran out for remnants of German LXIV Corps who had been trekking across France, hounded by the FFI. After taking Chalon, as French II Corps moved through the Beaune area, they came across over 1,000 men of 16. Infantry and 159. Reserve divisions and six trains stuffed with troops and weapons.

Opposite, Above and Below: *Occupational hazard—another downed bridge, this one over the Doubs at Besançon. The Germans were finding it difficult to set up a defensive line. Each time Wiese attempted to set up a coordinated defense, it collapsed. While there were occasional Allied reverses—such as at Baume-les-Dames where elements of the French 3e DIA were mauled—most of Nineteenth Army defenses folded quickly. At Besançon—ordered to hold to September 15, the battle was over by the 8th. 3rd Infantry Division assaulted the city's five surrounding Vauban forts and finally 1/30th Infantry captured the Citadel (for which they received a Presidential Unit Citation) with help from 9th Field Artillery and C/756 Tank Bn. The defenders—159. Infantry-Division—lost 250 dead and 2,500 captured; 3rd Division lost 80 dead with 90 wounded. The Germans fell back, hoping to set up a coordinated defense line centered on Vesoul.*

Above: *In good spirits—3rd Division's 7th Infantry Regiment at Larnod southwest of Besançon.*

Below and Bottom: *M4A4 Duguay-Trouin of 2RC from 1DB was knocked out by an antitank gun near Beaune on September 6. Hit by two rounds from around 1,000 yards, three of the crew were killed.*

LA PREMIERE ARMEE FRANÇAISE
COMMANDEE PAR
LE GENERAL DE LATTRE DE TASSIGNY
FORGEE EN AFRIQUE ET EN ITALIE
DEBARQUEE EN PROVENCE
GROSSIE DES FORCES FRANÇAISES
DE L'INTERIEUR
A LIBERE DIJON LE 11.9.1944
DANS SA MARCHE VICTORIEUSE
AU RHIN ET AU DANUBE

A week after Lyon fell, French II Corps was at the gates of Dijon. With Vesoul chosen as the next attempt to create a defensive line, there was little point fighting for Dijon, so the Germans abandoned the city. The plaque remembering the event (**Left**) on the outside wall of Jardin Darcy says: "French First Army commanded by Général de Lattre de Tassigny forged in Africa and Italy, landed in Provence, enlarged by the FFI liberated Dijon on September 11, 1944, during its victorious journey to the Rhine and Danube."

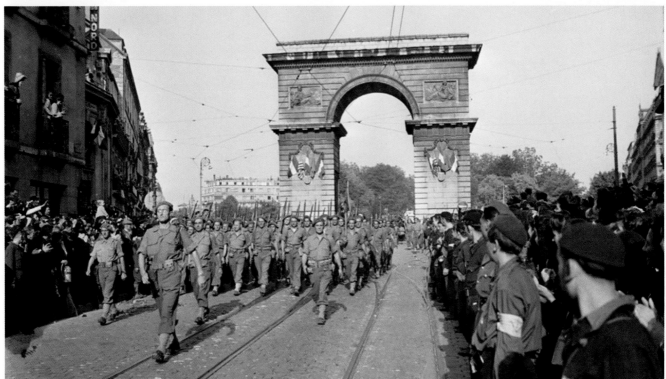

ICI LE 12 SEPTEMBRE 1944
S'OPERA LA JONCTION DES DEUX ANCIENNES DIVISIONS FRANCAISES
LIBRES LA 1ERE D.F.L ET LA 2EME D.B ELEMENTS AVANCES DES
FORCES LIBERATRICES DEBARQUEES EN PROVENCE ET EN NORMANDIE

BIR HAKEIM — KOUFRA
EL ALAMEIN — TUNISIE
TUNISIE — ALENCON
ITALIE — PARIS
PROVENCE — STRASBOURG
·ALSACE — BERGSTESGADEN

FRANCE LIBRE

18 JUIN 1940   8 MAI 1945

Opposite, Above: *Handshakes as recon units of US Third and Seventh armies meet at Autun. Although purporting to be the first handshake, they took place some days later, on the 13th: there had been meetings since the 10th.*

Opposite, Center and Below: *Monument in Nod-sur-Seine where, on September 12, 1DFL (Seventh) and 2DB (Third) met. Côte d'Or Tourisme (c) R. Guiton*

Above and Inset: *The Germans' attempt to create a defensive line centered on Vesoul didn't last. 3rd Division fought a tough battle, but with 36th Division threatening to get involved, LXIV Corps evacuated on the 12th. A lot has changed, but the stone parapet is the same on Vesoul's bridge over the Columbine river.*

Right: *A 756th Tank Battalion Sherman knocked out during the battle around Vesoul, September 14.*

Above and Left:
Casualty evacuation is difficult when the enemy is being pursued so rapidly. the "Green Book" reported: "During this period, clearing stations made almost daily moves, platoons leaping one another, while evacuation hospitals were hastily brought up to the combat area ... collecting stations were in almost continuous movement."

Opposite, Below:
Between them German demolition and Allied bombing had damaged a great deal of the French railroad system—particularly bridges and viaducts. Rebuilding was an essential aid to transporting matériel up the Rhône Valley. But what an effort was needed: 42 new bridges and over 800 miles of track. It was a massive and underrated achievement that saw rail movement from southern ports increase from 23% in September (of c. 130,000 tons) to 40% (of 554,000) in November. This viaduct is at Xertigny.

Left: *By mid-September the sunny summer days of Provence were a long way behind. This bogged M10 isn't going anywhere quickly.*

Below: *The Memorial to the Resistance at Dounoux is a Parc du souvenir made up of many stones, a monument, a Cross of Lorraine, and an arboretum.*

6 BELFORT AND STRASBOURG

Excellent study of an M7 HMC firing on German positions in the
Rhine Valley in December—the litter of shell cases shows the size
of the fire missions. By the beginning of September VI Corps had
advanced from the Riviera to the Moselle in less than a month. They
were getting tired and artillery was playing an increasingly important
role.

Opposite, Above: *The 76mm M1 gun took a long time to reach front-line troops who desperately needed harder-hitting firepower to combat the increased number of Panthers. The gun was developed in 1942, the mount in 1943, and it was not until July 1944 that the gun was accepted for combat. Here in Brouvelieures on October 29 the 756th Tank Battalion is issued with some of the new tanks but it will take until February 1945 until there are more 76mm-armed M4s in the battalion than 75mm.*

Below: *In the fall of 1944 the M1943 combat uniform—tested by 3rd Infantry Division in Italy earlier in the year—was issued to the troops. Here men of 157th Infantry Regiment (45th Division) try it out, seemingly oblivious to the dead German at their feet. The uniform jacket buttoned up under a flap giving a smooth front, and a hood could be attached. There were also matching trousers and cap, an inner pile jacket, and "combat boots" whose extra leather flap and double buckle tabs for standard ankle boots replaced canvas leggings.*

The handshakes between men of Third and Seventh Army gave the Allies a broad front from Switzerland to the English Channel. For two months, since Operation Cobra had broken the stalemate, the Germans had been in retreat: now the defense was beginning to thicken up. Closer to the German border their supply lines were easier and reinforcements and new equipment was forthcoming.

The tide of Allied success was beginning to ebb: Operation Market Garden would prove a bridge too far; First Army was soon to reach the borders of the Reich but would find Aachen a tough nut to crack; Patton's largely unopposed march through France had ground to a halt at Metz; Seventh Army's race up the Rhône had reached the difficult terrain of the Vosges Mountains—a much easier defensive position for the beleaguered Nineteenth Army who could no longer trade space for time to set up a defense. Having lost 40 percent of its August 15 strength, Nineteenth Army was on the ropes. Over 12,000 prisoners had been taken between September 3 and 14, mainly around Dijon. 11. Panzer, relatively intact at Lyon, had lost significant numbers of men and tanks in early September.

On the other hand, the Allies were also showing signs of fatigue. Logistics problems had seen most of the infantry cover most of the advance on foot. Casualties, light at first, had begun to mount: VI Corps had lost 2,050 killed, captured, or missing out of 9,900 casualties. The French had lost more—heavy urban fighting in Toulon and Marseille had contributed; the lightly armed FFI had also suffered badly. The speed of the advance and the lack of German resistance had more than outstripped the logistical practicalities: civilian shortages compounded by the retreating Germans meant that civilian relief was necessary. And the weather was getting autumnal. That meant rain and cold, swollen rivers, and trench foot.

There was another material change: no longer were Patch, Truscott, and de Lattre part of the Mediterranean Theater under distant command. Just as VI Corps was about to deal—Truscott hoped—a deadly blow on Nineteenth Army and force the Belfort Gap, SHAEF ordered all operations to stop. Eisenhower took over control of the southern forces on September 15 and was now handling the overall strategy and forcing the Belfort Gap wasn't, at that moment, a priority. At the same time, Sixth Army Group became operational, and command of XII TAC passed to Ninth Air Force.

Continued on p.161.

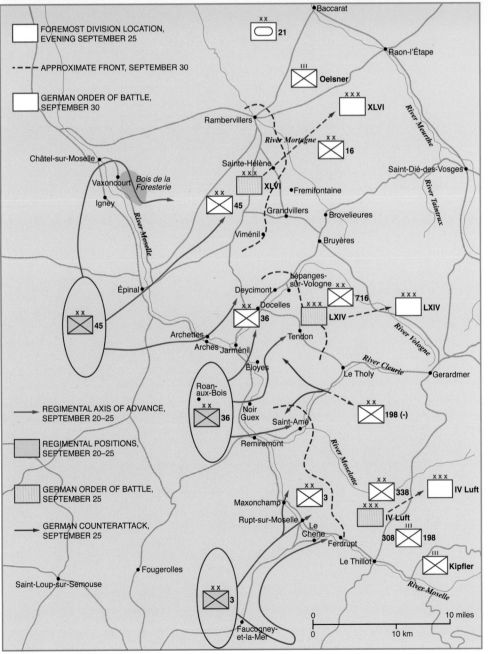

**FOREMOST DIVISION LOCATION,
EVENING SEPTEMBER 25**

APPROXIMATE FRONT, SEPTEMBER 30

**GERMAN ORDER OF BATTLE,
SEPTEMBER 30**

**REGIMENTAL AXIS OF ADVANCE,
SEPTEMBER 20–25**

**REGIMENTAL POSITIONS,
SEPTEMBER 20–25**

**GERMAN ORDER OF BATTLE,
SEPTEMBER 25**

**GERMAN COUNTERATTACK,
SEPTEMBER 25**

Left: *When SHAEF took over
the operational control of the
Dragoon forces, there were
immediate changes. First, the
two corps of French Armée B
were brought together on the
right flank of the Allied lines and
Army B became French First
Army. Patch argued strongly
that Seventh Army needed more
muscle—rather than just one
corps—but was refused more
men. In fact, Eisenhower would
have dearly liked to combine
Sixth and Twelfth army groups
but worried about how the
French would react. He had
sufficient "coalition problems"
dealing with the British 21st
Army Group and didn't fancy
exacerbating matters if de Gaulle
decided that the French forces
should be separate. Apart,
therefore, from the change of XII
TAC's command structure and
the physical positioning of his
forces, Devers was allowed some
independence—made easier by
the logistical highway back to
the Mediterranean ports and the
remarkable railroad infrastructure
repairs that were ongoing. Held
until September 19, by which
time the French redeployment
south was well advanced,
Truscott's VI Corps was ready
to cross the Moselle. In front of
him, German Nineteenth Army
had been weakened almost to
disintegration and Army Group
G, after the failure of Manteuffel's
counterattack in Lorraine,
had a new commander as
Generalleutnant Hermann Balck
replaced Blaskowitz.*

155

Above and Opposite: *The Moselle Offensive saw 45th Division attack in the north centered on Épinal; the 36th towards Eloyes and Remiremont; and the 3rd towards Rupt. The 3rd started in Faucogney-et-la-Mer—a commune in the southwest corner of the Vosges noted for its 1,000 lakes, difficult terrain to negotiate. As the offensive began, 3rd Infantry got over the Moselle at Rupt and Ferdrupt easily enough but then ran into problems. Divisional commander, Maj Gen John E. O'Daniel saw the 7th Infantry cross the Moselle but the 30th ran into trouble in the southeast. Once French troops had moved up to protect their flank, the 30th moved north over the Moselle. This is C Co 1/7th Infantry in Faucogney.*

Below: *The 45th got across the river unmolested, held the bridgehead long enough for engineers to erect bridges, and then moved east. Here, an M4 of 191st Tank Bn at Les Arches crossing the Moselle to give support to 3/179th Infantry, the southerly arm of 45th Division's attack.*

VOSGES MEMORIALS

Piquante Pierre is one of the highest peaks in the Vosges near Basse-sur-le-Rupt, and it was the base for a Maquis that was attacked on September 19–21 by the Germans. The memorial names the 83 Maquisards who died—although it is reported that there were nearly 500 German casualties in a battle that took place high up and for most of the time in heavy fog. © Christian Amet/WikiCommons (CC BY 2.5)

Bottom: La Croix des Monats is a memorial to the Moroccan Goumiers of French First Army who fought here. Sapin88/WikiCommons (CC BY-SA 3.0)

Opposite: *The 157th Infantry, 45th Division's northern attack, had been slowed up by mines and roadblocks and couldn't find a crossing and so headed north to use a Third Army bridge in place in Chatel. Further south, 3/157th crossed the Canal de l'Est (**Opposite, Center**) running to the west of the Moselle and the river itself (**Opposite, Above and Below**) near Igney on September 22. The 45th's progress ground to a halt in heavy fighting in the Bois de la Foresterie until the 24th when continued pressure bore fruit and the German position collapsed.*

Right: *The attack on Épinal by the 180th Infantry was hindered when the Germans blew the final bridge, but secured the city on the 24th and a Bailey bridge was quickly built. Photo shows AAA defenses on the Moselle just upriver from the Bailey bridge.*

Top and Above: *September was a good time to cross the Moselle. By November 8 the rains had swelled the river to a torrent that came close to compromising the bridge.*

By September 30 VI Corps had advanced well past the Moselle and, allied to Third Army pressure to the north, the German line was forced to retreat, the elements opposite VI Corps moving back into the Vosges Mountains.

GO FOR BROKE!

"Rarely has a nation been so well served by a people it has so ill-treated." When Japan bombed Pearl Harbor, all American men of Japanese descent whether Japanese or born in the United States—the Nisei—became enemy aliens. 110,000 were interned. This wasn't practical in Hawaii where nearly half the population was of Japanese ancestry. When the 442nd Regimental Combat Team was set up huge numbers—particularly in Hawaii—tried to join. The 442nd RCT performed with outstanding bravery during the war—9,486 Purple Hearts, 4,000 Bronze Stars, 560 Silver Stars, 33 Distinguished Service Crosses, 21 Medals of Honor, seven Presidential Unit Citations, and many more. 20 of the Medals of Honor were upgraded from lesser medals in 2000 by President Bill Clinton.

On October 24, 1/141st Infantry (36th Division) was sent to a position near Biffontaine where it was cut off. An attempt to save them using the rest of the regiment and attached tanks failed. So the divisional commander, General Dahlquist, sent in the Nisei who got the job done but paid a terrible price. In three weeks fighting from their attachment to the Texas Division on October 13 the unit lost 140 killed, 1,800 wounded, and 43 missing. In October 1963, Texas Governor John Connally declared all members of the RCT honorary Texan citizens for helping save 211 men of 1/141st.

Above Left: *Congressional Gold Medal awarded to the 100th Infantry Battalion, the 442nd Regimental Combat Team, and the Military Intelligence Service—segregated military units of Japanese descent who fought with the US Army—on November 2, 2011.*

Left: *Two color guards and color bearers of the Japanese-American 442nd Combat Team, stand at attention during a medal ceremony, while the citations are read. They are standing on ground in the Bruyères area, France, where many of their comrades fell. November 12, 1944.*

On September 22 Eisenhower called a conference of the major Allied leaders. During this he agreed to an attack through Belfort on Strasbourg. He also agreed to move one of Patton's corps to Sixth Army Group—the XV under the command of Maj Gen Wade H. Haislip. He would also allocate six divisions either already in or about to join Bradley's 12th Army Group during September and October. Patton's reaction was less sanguine than Bradley's: "May God rot his guts." This windfall netted Patch over 50,000 troops which included US 79th Division, French 2DB, 106th Cavalry Group, and various corps troops. As important was the quality of the units and their leaders: XV Corps had distinguished itself under Patton, as had Leclerc and his armor. The only problem was that XV Corps had been in action for over three months and didn't arrive without baggage: its infantry regiments were short of men; 2DB's tanks needed an overhaul; and their logistical problems mirrored everyone else's. On top of this, while coming under Sixth Army Group's control, it was still to perform its obligations protecting Third Army's southern flank and other tactical missions already in train—including 79th Division's slugging match in the Parroy Forest, which took from September 25 to October 9.

While these new units were fulfilling their existing duties, VI Corps pushed on again, with the 45th leading and reaching the River Mortagne and Grandvillers. The 3rd, however, was finding the going tough: fighting in the Vosges mountains in dismal weather affected morale and fighting spirit.

While 79th Division cleared Parroy Forest, VI Corps' northern flank was exposed. However, Patch and Truscott didn't want to sit still and let the Germans develop their defenses and so planned an attack towards Saint-Dié-des-Vosges—Operation Dogface. The first step of this was to take Brouvelieures and Bruyères. The 45th Division attacked and made progress until counterattacked by units of 11. Panzer. To the southeast, 36th Division supported the attack, the 141st Regiment bearing the brunt against German 716. Division. Further south 3rd Division attacked toward Le Tholy, Vagney, and Seppois. Fighting in the Vosges, with its steep valleys and forests, was hard work and while 30th Infantry had made relatively good progress, casualties were been high.

On October 25 Truscott took command of Fifth Army in Italy and his post was taken by Maj Gen Edward H. Brookes. "Dogface" was continued. It was a slugging match in the harsh terrain, poor weather, and dense forests. Both sides suffered casualties, but the Germans just held on. During this period 1/141st Infantry became isolated and surrounded. Short on supplies—they even received canisters fired by artillery—the 442nd Regiment of Japanese-Americans finally effected their rescue, but at great cost. By the time it was pulled out of the line the 442nd could call on less than half its authorized strength.

Opposite, Below: *During the autumn rains keeping the roads open was a major problem. This is 45th Division's 36th Engineer Battalion in Fraispertuis.*

Below: *At Vagney, on October 7, 2Lt James Harris of A Coy 756th Tank Battalion won a posthumous Congressional Medal of Honor while defending 3/7th Infantry's HQ from attack.*

Bottom, Left and Right: *Brouvelieures seen on October 29, a week after it had been taken by 179th Infantry (45th Division) after house-to-house fighting.*

Opposite, Above: *VI Corps' role in the November offensive was predicated on a successful completion to Operation Dogface. In the first week of November, therefore, 45th Division continued to batter its way through the forests towards Saint-Dié. It didn't quite get there, but it had got close to the west bank of the Meurthe before being pulled out of the line, exhausted. 3rd Division had reached the banks of the Meurthe and two of its regiments would go into reserve. Their places would be taken by new divisions: US 100th Infantry Division (CG Maj Gen Withers A. Burrell) and 103rd (Maj Gen Charles C. Haffner).*

Right: *La Salle near Rambervillers on November 3. This is where a PzKpfw IV round penetrated this 45th Division M4A1 killing two of the crew.*

Below: *Memorial to the "Cotton Balers"—7th Infantry of 3rd Division—who fought a bitter battle against German Gebirgsjäger who were trying to stem the drive toward Saint-Dié on Hautes Jacques. The four-day stalemate was broken by Co E 2/7th.*

Below Right: *Flooded positions in the Les Rouges Eaux area, November 8, as M4s of 756th Tank Bn were used as artillery.*

Opposite, Below: *Sturmgeschütz IIIG (note Saukopf cast mantlet) KO'd by a 36th Infantry Division M4(76) at Saint-Crox-aux-Mines on November 28.*

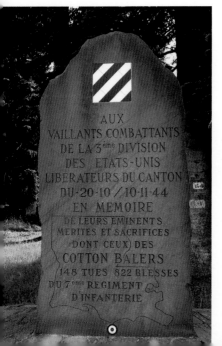

The November Offensive

VI Corps' October attacks had ground down the German defenses and left Sixth Army Group poised to roll up the German line. A general offensive was planned to start in mid-November. From the north, XV Corps would attack through the Saverne Gap (see p. 169); VI Corps would finish "Dogface" and then attack through Saint-Dié and the Saales Pass toward Strasbourg; while French II Corps would support "Dogface" and then thrust toward Gerardmer in support of VI Corps and to help keep German units in place. The main French attack would be by I Corps aiming for Mulhouse through the Belfort Gap (see p. 164), although a last-minute political decision by de Gaulle to use First Army troops to clear the Gironde and La Rochelle—although it didn't happen—complicated matters.

The key to this offensive was Baccarat, which gave both a crossing of the River Meurthe and access to the Saverne Gap. XV Corps entrusted this job to Leclerc's 2DB—at first glance an odd choice because the weather and mud would seem to negate the benefits of armor. In fact, Leclerc performed brilliantly, seizing Baccarat and the bridge for minimal losses.

VI Corps—reinforced with new divisions—was faced by a German army that was in tatters. Adept at defense, using mines, booby-traps, and artillery, but above all making use of the terrain, most of their units were low on strength and morale, although their artillery was in good order.

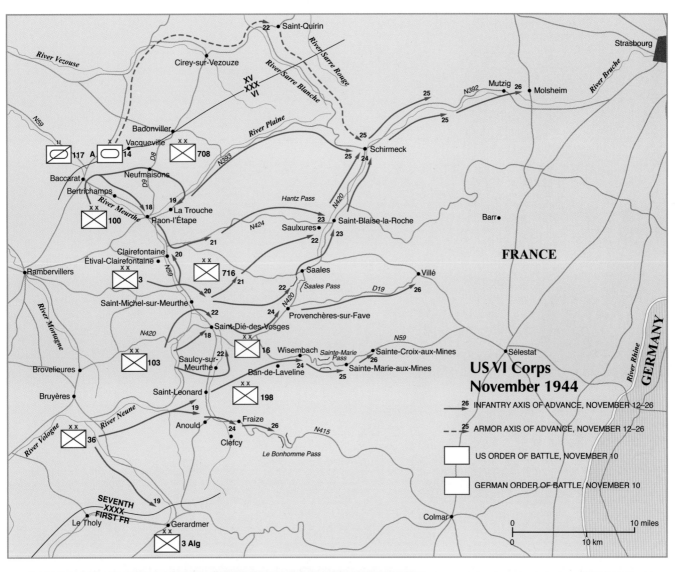

US VI Corps
November 1944

Map labels and features:

Strasbourg

River Vezouse

Saint-Quirin
Cirey-sur-Vezouze
River Sarre Rouge
River Sarre Blanche

XV
XXX
VI

Badonviller
River Plaine

N59
Vacqueville
117 A 14
708

Neufmaisons
Baccarat
Bertrichamps
River Meurthe
La Trouche
100
Raon-l'Étape

Mutzig
Molsheim
N392
River Bruche

Schirmeck
Hantz Pass
N420

Barr
FRANCE

Clairefontaine
Étival-Clairefontaine
Rambervillers
N59
3
716
N424
Saulxures
Saint-Blaise-la-Roche

Saint-Michel-sur-Meurthe
Saales
Saales Pass
D19
Villé

River Mortagne
Broveleures
103
N420
Saulcy-sur-Meurthe
Saint-Dié-des-Vosges
16
Wisembach
Provenchères-sur-Fave

Sélestat

Bruyères
Saint-Leonard
198
Ban-de-Laveline
Sainte-Marie Pass
Sainte-Croix-aux-Mines
N59
Sainte-Marie-aux-Mines

River Neune
River Vologne
36
Anould
Fraize
Clefcy
Le Bonhomme Pass
N415

GERMANY
River Rhine

SEVENTH
XXXX
FIRST FR
Le Tholy
Gerardmer
3 Alg

Colmar

26 → INFANTRY AXIS OF ADVANCE, NOVEMBER 12–26
25 --- ARMOR AXIS OF ADVANCE, NOVEMBER 12–26
□ US ORDER OF BATTLE, NOVEMBER 10
□ GERMAN ORDER OF BATTLE, NOVEMBER 10

0 ____ 10 miles
0 ____ 10 km

The Belfort Gap

DÉLIVRANCE

METZ NOVEMBRE 1944
MULHOUSE NOV. 1944
STRASBOURG NOV. 1944
COLMAR FÉVRIER 1945

NUMÉRO SPÉCIAL
SUR LA DÉLIVRANCE DE L'ALSACE ET DE LA LORRAINE
ÉDITÉ PAR LA DIRECTION DES SERVICES DE PRESSE DU MINISTÈRE DE LA GUERRE

12 FRANCS

Opposite, Above: *French progress in the southern Vosges had been minimal in late September and October thanks to foul weather and staunch German defense—particularly accurate artillery fire. With 1DB rested and fully equipped, as part of a concerted attack along the entire Sixth Army Group Front, de Lattre's men finally cut loose—including Maj Gen du Touzet du Vigier's 1DB (to his surprise: he had been expecting to head off to the Gironde). By 18:00 on November 19, French forces were on the Rhine at Rosenau.*

Above: Déliverance: *a Free French magazine produced in 1945 remembers the liberation of the great cities of eastern France.* Art Media/Print Collector/Getty Images

1 *Distinctive French helmets on the Vosges Front, November 1944.* LAPI/Roger Viollet/Getty Images.

2 *Lefebvre barracks in Mulhouse, November 27.* LAPI/Roger Viollet/Getty Images

3 and 4 *French First Army 105mm artillery.* LAPI/Roger Viollet/Getty Images

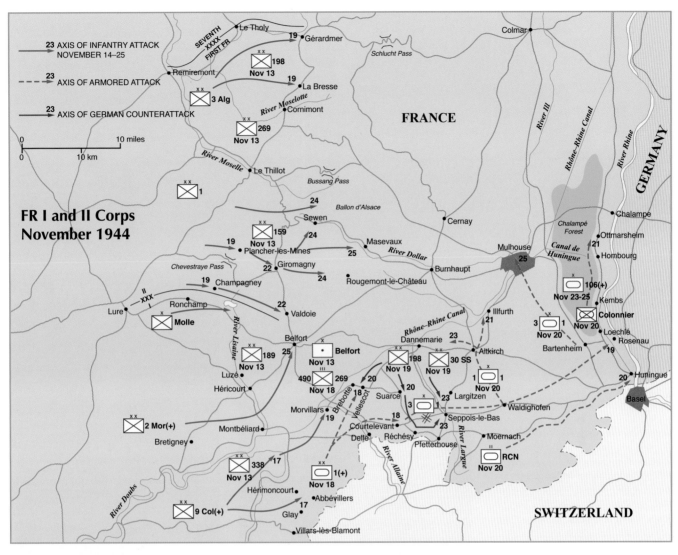

FR I and II Corps
November 1944

Legend:
- 23 → AXIS OF INFANTRY ATTACK NOVEMBER 14–25
- 23 ⇢ AXIS OF ARMORED ATTACK
- 23 → AXIS OF GERMAN COUNTERATTACK

Scale: 0 – 10 miles / 0 – 10 km

FRANCE

GERMANY

SWITZERLAND

Le Tholy, Gérardmer, Colmar, Schlucht Pass, Remiremont, 198 Nov 13, 19, La Bresse, 3 Alg, River Moselotte, Cornimont, 269 Nov 13, River Ill, Rhône–Rhine Canal, River Rhine, Chalampé, 1, Le Thillot, Bussang Pass, Chalampé Forest, Ottmarsheim, Sewen, Ballon d'Alsace, 24, 21, Hombourg, 159 Nov 13, 24, Masevaux, Cernay, Canal de Huningue, Plancher-les-Mines, 25, River Dollar, Mulhouse, 25, 106(+) Nov 23-25, Kembs, Chevestraye Pass, 22, Giromagny, 24, Burnhaupt, Rougemont-le-Château, Champagney, 19, Valdoie, Rhône–Rhine Canal, Illfurth, 21, 3 1 Nov 20, Colonnier Nov 20, Loechlé, Rosenau, Lure, Ronchamp, Molle, River Lisaine, Belfort, Dannemarie, 23, Altkirch, Bartenheim, 19, 189 Nov 13, Belfort Nov 13, 198 Nov 19, 30 SS Nov 19, 1 1 Nov 20, 20, Huningue, Luzé, 490 269 Nov 18, 20, Suarce, 20, Largitzen, Waldighofen, Basel, Héricourt, Brébotte, Vellescot, 18, 23, 3 1, 2 Mor(+), Morvillars, 19, Courtelevant, 18, Seppois-le-Bas, 23, Montbéliard, Delle, Réchésy, Pfetterhouse, Moernach, River Largue, RCN Nov 20, Bretigney, 338 Nov 13, 17, 1(+) Nov 18, River Alaine, River Doubs, 9 Col(+), Hérimoncourt, 17, Abbévillers, Glay, Villars-lès-Blamont

Above: *Rosenau is where French First Army reached the Rhine in the form of Lt Jean de Loisy. This M4A1E8 is a memorial to the events of November 19.*

Above Right: *The 2e Zouaves were given the name Magenta after for their role in the 1859 battle.*

Right and Far right: *Memorials in Seppois-les-Bas, the first village liberated in Alsace. On November 19 a detachment of RICM, the recon regiment of the 9DIC, pushed through the village over the Largue River, losing a tank on the way. There are memorials including the RICM (**Right**) and RIM (**Far right**).*

Below: *M4A2* Cornouailles *in Belfort. The turret is original. On November 21 around 17:30,* Cornouailles *was supporting 10/4RTM in an attack on Belfort's Fort de la Miotte when it was hit by an antitank round. While trying to extricate his vehicle, the tank commander Lt Martin of 6RCA, was killed.*

Above and Right: *Into Belfort. The French didn't have it all their own way—1,300 dead of 6,000 casualties; 85 tanks and TDs destroyed. The German counterattack of November 20–23 cut the N463 and the supply route to the advanced units. Two groups, one built around elements of 198. Division (Grenadier-Regiment 308) and the other 30. SS-Division, pushed toward Seppois. At the same time, reinforcements in the shape of Stürmgeschütz-Brigade 280 and Panzer-Brigade 106 Feldherrnhalle were supposed support the attack. Feldherrnhalle came too late—StuG-Bde 280 not at all—and was engaged and held by 1DB. The 308. Grenadier roadblock was smashed and what was left of the unit escaped into Switzerland.*

Below: *M4A4 Austerlitz of 2RCA (1DB) which took part in the liberation of Mulhouse and was knocked out by a Panzerfaust on November 23. The commander, Lt Jean de Loisy, remembered at Rosenau, was killed.* Rémi Stosskopf/WikiCommons

Below Right: *One of a series of plaques that mark the path of French First Army (see also p. 147).*

LA PREMIERE ARMEE FRANCAISE
COMMANDEE PAR
LE GENERAL DE LATTRE DE TASSIGNY
FORGEE EN AFRIQVE ET EN ITALIE
DEBARQVEE EN PROVENCE
GROSSIE DES FORCES FRANCAISES
DE L INTERIEVR
A LIBERE BELFORT LE 20·II·1944
DANS SA MARCHE VICTORIEVSE
AV RHIN ET AV DANVBE

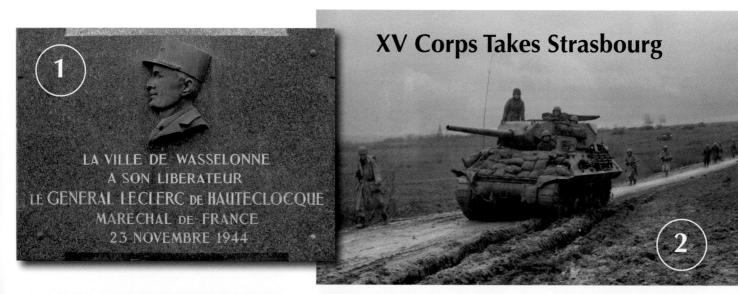

LA VILLE DE WASSELONNE
A SON LIBERATEUR
LE GENERAL LECLERC DE HAUTECLOCQUE
MARECHAL DE FRANCE
23 NOVEMBRE 1944

XV Corps Takes Strasbourg

PASSANT QUI QUE TU SOIS, ARRETE-TOI
RESPECTUEUSEMENT DEVANT CE CHAR
DU 501ème REGIMENT DE CHARS DE COMBAT
DE LA 2ème DIVISION BLINDEE COMMANDEE
PAR LE GENERAL LECLERC FRAPPE ICI
A L'ENNEMI LE 17 NOVEMBRE 1944
EN LIBÉRANT BADONVILLER

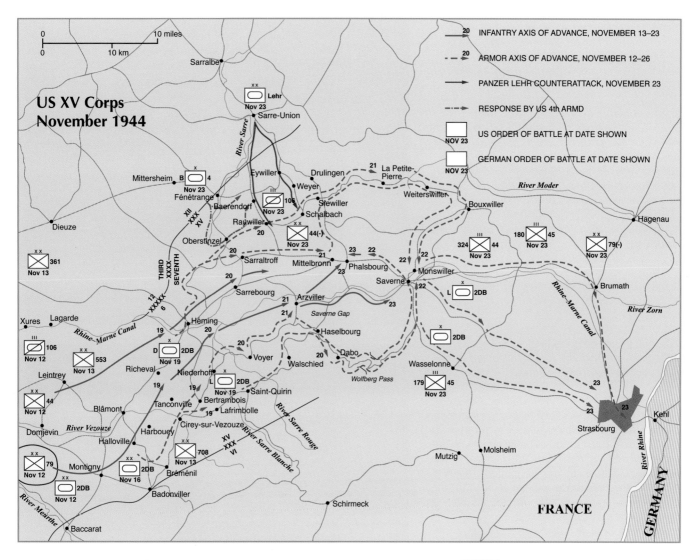

**US XV Corps
November 1944**

0 _____ 10 miles
0 _____ 10 km

⟶ 20 INFANTRY AXIS OF ADVANCE, NOVEMBER 13–23

⟶ 20 ARMOR AXIS OF ADVANCE, NOVEMBER 12–26

⟶ PANZER LEHR COUNTERATTACK, NOVEMBER 23

⟶ RESPONSE BY US 4th ARMD

☐ NOV 23 US ORDER OF BATTLE AT DATE SHOWN

☐ NOV 23 GERMAN ORDER OF BATTLE AT DATE SHOWN

FRANCE

GERMANY

(7)

Above: *XV Corps' advance on November 12–23 took Devers' Sixth Army Group to Strasbourg through the Saverne Gap. Four divisions were involved: 44th, 79th, and 106th Infantry Divisions and Leclerc's 2DB. After initial slow going, by the 18th the battle was more fluid and Haislip let 2DB off the leash. Divided into combat commands, CCD (Colonel Louis Dio), CCL (Colonel de Langlade), CCR (Colonel Jean Remy) and CCV (Colonel Pierre Billotte), they made their way into Strasbourg to make good the promise that Leclerc and his men had made in Koufra, North Africa.*

1 *The main prize for the French in general, and Leclerc in particular, was Strasbourg—the subject of the Koufra oath. There are numerous monuments and plaques that remember the general and his 2DB, including this one at Wasselonne.* Ctruongngoc/WikiCommons (CC BY-SA 3.0)

2 *M10 of 2DB negotiates the mud outside Halloville on November 13.*

3 and 4 *Mort-Homme was knocked out on November 17 and was placed to commemorate the liberation of Badonviller by 501RCC French General Leclerc.* Bertranfenne/WikiCommons (CC BY-SA 3.0)

5 and 6 *A mishap at Saverne. Today the railroad bridge is preserved as part of a roundabout.*

7 *Another 2DB Sherman, this one M4A3 Bourg-la-Reine of 12RC at Phalsbourg. Knocked out on November 23, it was saved on Leclerc's express orders to act as a memorial.*

1 and 2 *French armor in Strasbourg. CCL entered the city at 10:30 on the 23rd, CCV from 13:00 along with 313th Infantry (79th Division). By the time they left on November 28, they had taken 6,000 prisoners.*

3 *M4A3* Cherbourg *on the Route du Rhin in Strasbourg. The fount of all knowledge on surviving tanks (Surviving Panzers) points out that this name was actually used by an M4A3 armed with a 105mm (this one has a 75mm) of 12RC knocked out here in November 1944. Another 2DB Sherman named* Meknès *was also knocked out close by.*

4 *Memorial to fallen World War II US troops inside Strasbourg cathedral.*
W. B. Wilson/WikiCommons (CC BY 2.5)

5 and 6 *Leclerc salutes a parade of 12RC on Place Kléber on November 26. Behind him is his faithful aide-de-camp Christian Girard.*

7, 8, and 9 *Parts of Strasbourg center survived unharmed, although the area the Germans held near the Rhine was badly damaged.*

While French eyes were on Strasbourg, OBW Gerd von Rundstedt realized that only a successful counterattack was going to retrieve the position for the Germans. Panzer Lehr was refitting behind the battlefield and had been earmarked for use in the Ardennes Offensive, but on November 21 OKH finally gave permission to use it until the 28th when it would have to go north. Von Rundstedt urged Balck to attack XV Corps' flank (see map p. 169). The German armor—some 34 PzKpfw IVs and 38 Panthers—moved slowly into position and received little assistance from other German units on the ground: they were too weakened already or too involved. The attack when it came—late on the 23rd—pushed southeast to Rauwiller and Schalbach, but soon von Rundstedt realized that it wasn't going to work. What he didn't know was that things were just about to get critical. US 4th Armored had moved over the Sarre River and was hitting Panzer Lehr in the flank at Baerendorf. By the 25th it was all over. The attack by 4th Armored and accurate, intensive artillery fire sent Panzer Lehr away to lick its wounds. It resurfaced in the Ardennes advancing to Rochefort before being beaten back. It was then heavily involved trying to cut the corridor to Bastogne created by ... US 4th Armored, who had spearheaded Third Army's advance.

A LA MEMOIRE
DES OFFICIERS, SOUS-OFFICIERS
ET SOLDATS AMERICAINS TOMBES
SUR LE SOL D'ALSACE POUR SA
LIBERATION

1944-1945

IN MEMORY
OF THE AMERICAN OFFICERS
NON COMMISSIONED OFFICERS
AND SOLDIERS WHO GAVE
THEIR LIFE
TO FREE ALSACE

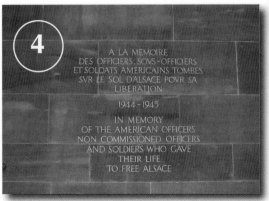

Leclerc's serment de Koufra, March 2, 1941

"Nous sommes en marche, nous ne arrêtons que lorsque le drapeau français flottera sur la cathédrale de Strasbourg."

"We are on the march, we will only stop when the French flag floats over Strasbourg cathedral."

7 OPERATION NORDWIND

75th Division on the snow-covered Colmar Plain during the battle to break down the Colmar Pocket. Note the snow camouflage on the tanks. "Nordwind"—North Wind—was well named as January 1945 was Arctic: the wet, cold, gray weather of December had given way to freezing temperatures and snow.

Above: *Reports of an enemy tank column sends Allied armor to meet them with a 275th Infantry Regiment 57mm anti-tank gun guarding the road into Phillipsbourg.*

Opposite, Above: *The Germans concentrated what—on paper at least—was a strong force. However, many of the units were considerably smaller than their titles suggest: 25. Panzer-grenadier-Division was no more than a strengthened regiment as was 36. Volksgrenadier-Division. Nevertheless, there were a number of good units with good morale. As was usual for the German military, however, the command structure was a major disadvantage: Army Group Oberrhein was placed under the command of Heinrich Himmler who proved a poor choice. Blaskowitz, who had once again taken over command of Army Group G, wanted longer to prepare and Oberrhein units involved in supporting attacks to come under his command. Hitler would allow neither.*

Following the collapse of Panzer Lehr's counterattack, one of the great "what ifs" of World War II now presented itself to the Allies. With Sixth Army Group's routing of the German forces facing them and a Rhine crossing beckoning, Devers' two armies had created an opportunity that did not exist in front of 12th and 21st army groups who faced a more organized foe backed by the integrated defenses of the Westwall. There was an opportunity to cross the Rhine and thrust deep into German territory. However, to Devers' and Patch's dismay, Eisenhower and Bradley were more concerned to do something about "Patton's flagging offensive"— although there was little they could do about the awful weather, non-battle injuries (mainly trench foot), and the strength of the Westwall.

Had the Sixth Army Group attacked over the Rhine the Germans may have had to curtail or stop the Ardennes operation and they would not have been able to build up their forces in the Colmar Pocket—but the opportunity passed. Instead, in early December the Allies advanced north to the German border, forcing Nineteenth Army back to the Westwall, and the French were tasked with breaking down the Colmar Pocket. And then, on December 16, the Germans initiated the surprise offensive that became known as the Battle of the Bulge. Soon, Sixth Army Group's front-age increased substantially as Third Army wheeled to effect the rescue of Bastogne and reduction of the "bulge," and Devers had to send men and equipment north to help counter the German thrust: when Patton's 80th Infantry and 4th Armored divisions moved north the 12th Armored Division had to move north to fill in the gap left by their departure. On December 19, Eisenhower ordered Devers to stop offensive operations and even be prepared to pull back from some of the hard-won ground. This also meant that the attack on the Colmar Pocket stopped.

Then, to add to Devers' problems, on January 1 the Germans struck the stretched Sixth Army Group: Operation Nordwind had begun. Initially there were two attacks: at Rimling 100th Division held firm against

German Order of Battle

ARMY GROUP G (Generaloberst Johannes Blaskowitz till January 29; SS-Oberstgruppenführer Paul Hausser after)

First Army (Generalleutnant Hans von Obstfelder)

25. PzGr Division (Oberst Arnold Burmeister)

21. Pz Division (Generalleutnant Edgar Feuchtinger)

6. SS-Gebirgs Division Nord (SS-Gruppenfuhrer Karl Brenner)

XIII SS Corps (Obergruppenfiihrer-SS Max Simon)

19. VG Division (Generalleutnant Walter Wissmath)

36. VG Division (Generalmajor Helmut Kleikamp)

17. SS-PzGr Division *Götz von Berlichingen* (SS-Standartenfuhrer Hans Lingner)

XC Corps (General der Flieger Erich Petersen)

559. VG Division (Generalleutnant Kurt Freiherr von Muhlen)

257. VG Division (Generalmajor Erich Seidel)

LXXXIX Corps (General der Infanterie Gustav Höhne)

361. VG Division (Generalmajor Alfred Philippi)

245. Infanterie Division (Generalleutnant Erwin Sander)

256. VG Division (Generalmajor Gerhard Franz)

ARMY GROUP UPPER RHINE (Reichsführer-SS Heinrich Himmler)—dissolved January 29

Nineteenth Army (General der Infanterie Siegfried Rasp)

10. SS-Pz Division *Frundsberg* (SS-Brigadeführer Heinz Harmel)

LXIV Corps (General der Infanterie Helmut Thumm November 1, 1944–January 15, 1945; Generalleutnant Friedrich-Wilhelm Hauck January 15–21; General der Artillerie Maximilian Grimmeis January 21–April 15)

106. Infantry Division (Generalleutnant Werner Forst from December 30)

189. Infantry Division (Generalmajor Ernst von Bauer)

198. Infantry Division (Generalmajor Otto Schiel; from January 18 Generalmajor Konrad Barde)

708. VG Division (Generalmajor Wilhelm Bleckwenn)

LXIII Corps (General der Infanterie Erich Abraham)

159. Infantry Division (Generalmajor Heinrich Bürcky)

269. Infantry Division Generalleutnant Hans Wagner)

338. Infantry Division (Generalmajor Konrad Barde; from January 18 Generalmajor Wolf Ewert)

716. Infantry Division (Oberst Ernst von Bauer; Generalmajor Wolf Ewert December 30–January 18)

Sturmgeschütz-Brigade 280 (Hauptmann Fritz Sebald; Hauptmann Wilhelm Lechens from February 10)

schwere Panzerjäger-Abteilung 654 (Major Hermann Sachtleben)

Panzer-Brigade 106 *Feldherrnhalle* (Oberst Franze Bäke; Maj Bernhard von Schkopp January 12–24; Oberlt Soommer)

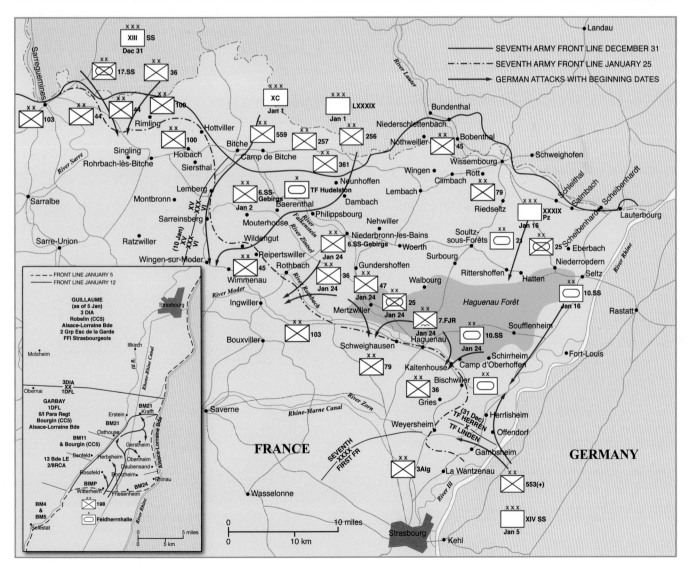

Above: *This French 2DB M7 has just finished firing 200 rounds near Witternheim (south of Strasbourg), December 24. The French position during December and January was complicated both by the personalities—their most successful and charismatic general, Philippe Leclerc, wanted to remain under US control rather than that of French First Army—and the politics: de Gaulle wanted the Atlantic coast fortresses which were still under German control retaken. Neither de Lattre nor Leclerc wanted to do this—it was militarily insignificant but there were still sizeable garrisons (11,500 in La Rochelle; 8,500 around the Gironde. The proposed operation was postponed a number of times during the fighting in Alsace and took place as Operation Venerable April 14–19, 1945.*

Below: *Soldiers seek shelter under a tank as counter-battery fire falls near the CP of 2/314th Infantry (79th Division) on January 6, 1945, at Rohrwiller (near Haguenau). The US forces in Alsace in 1945 were a mixture of the battle-hardened but battle-weary troops who had fought their way from Normandy or the Riviera, and fresh troops who were flooding into Europe from the United States. They were well led and better equipped than the Germans—although initially the provision of cold weather clothing could have been better—and they performed well: dogged in defense and more than a match for their enemies.*

XIII SS and LXXXIX corps; through Bitche the attack did better and the Germans introduced 6. SS-Gebirgs-Division *Nord*, but the US forces held firm. There were other major attacks: on the 5th by Himmler's Army Group Oberrhein at Rheinau and Gambesheim threatened Strasbourg; on the 7th Operation *Sonnenwende* (solstice), further south, also threatened Strasbourg; also on the 7th XXXIX Panzer Corps (temporarily Army Group G's reserve) attacked and for a time things got a bit hairy, particularly when the Germans reached the Haguenau Forest at Hatten and Rittershoffen. The Germans rushed reinforcements into the battle, 7.FJR attacking Hatten and Rittershoffen on January 10/11 and then XXXIX Panzer Corps was committed to the fray, with 10. SS-Panzer and 7.FJR divisions and Sturmgeschütz-Brigaden 384 and 667 advancing south down the Rhine, linking up with the Gambesheim attack.

On the night of January 20–21 the American forces withdrew to the Moder River. The reduced lines enabled VI Corps to withstand the final round of attacks initiated by the Germans on January 24/25. Held, the Germans ended the offensive and moved their best forces east. Blaskowitz was relieved of command and Paul Hausser took over.

This extremely brief summation of the month's fighting doesn't in any way convey what it was like to sit in a freezing trench being attacked by a fanatical enemy. There's no doubt that the Allies in Alsace were assisted later on by the successes in the Ardennes, which freed up men and matériel, but the main reasons for their success were the excellent organization of the defense by Maj Gen Ted Brookes (VI Corps' commander since Lucien Truscott's move to Italy) and the doggedness of the GIs in the field.

In mid-March US Seventh and French First armies went back on the offensive as Sixth Army Group was tasked with clearing northeast Alsace and establishing bridgeheads over the Rhine. Operation Undertone (March 15–25) did what was asked, but it didn't get a chance to inflict a heavy defeat on the enemy as German Army Group G fought delaying actions to allow the bulk of its forces to cross the Rhine to better defensive positions.

1 *57mm roadblock at Wingen, January 7. Attacked by 361.VGD and I. and III./SS-Gebirgsjäger-Regiment 12 (6. SS-Gebirgsjäger-Division) on January 3, 1/179th Infantry and nearby 276th Infantry were taken by surprise. Most of 179th—8 officers and 256 men—were taken prisoner. Initial counterattacks didn't work, but reinforcements—including a battalion of the 724th—accurate artillery fire, and house-to-house fighting on January 6–7 finally cleared the village and rescued the captives. The "green" 70th Division had performed well against the Gebirgsjäger and 2/274th received a Presidential Unit Citation.*

2 *A 14th Armored Division M4A3—heavily sandbagged for protection from Panzerfausts—is seen at Niederbetschdorf on its way to the Rittershoffen front, January 19. 14th Armored landed at Marseille on October 29 and took part in VI Corps' advance through the Vosges. In December, it crossed the Lauter River and was ready to advance into Germany before Eisenhower curtailed Seventh Army operations. During Nordwind, when the Germans tried to break through to Haguenau and Strasbourg, attacking at Rittershoffen and Hatten, 14th Armored—VI Corps' final reserve—fought an impressive defensive action January 9–21, 1945, against XXXIX Panzer Corps—supplemented from January 15 by FJR20 from the 7.FJR Division and the 104. Infantry from 47.VGD. The bravery of 14th Armored allowed Seventh Army time to move back to prepared positions along the Moder River, frustrated the German attacks, and saw it win two Presidential Unit Citations. Devers called it "one of the greatest defensive battles of the war."*

3 *Bischwiller 714th Tank Bn, 12th Armored Division ready to fire into Drusenheim January 8, 1945. The German attack across the Rhine north of Strasbourg was more successful than that in the south and created political problems for the Allies. The French refused to leave Strasbourg and in the end, they didn't.*

Ici tomberent le 4 fev. 1945 a 18 heures pour la liberation de l'Alsace le Brigadier-Chef Richard et le Spahi Sansoni du 4eme R.S.M. 1 Peloton. La ville de Rouffach reconnaissante.

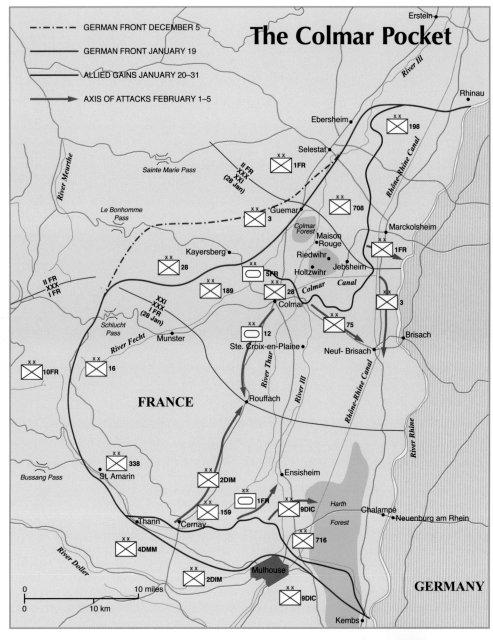

The Colmar Pocket

1 and 2 *Lt Audie Murphy showing off a chestful of medals, including the Congressional Medal of Honor round his neck. He was awarded it after the action at Holtzwihr where there is a memorial in the woods (*2*).*

3 *Rouffach memorial to Brig Chef Richard and Spahi Sansoni from 4RSMI who died here at 18:00 on February 4 during the fighting.*

4 *German PoWs escorted by French troops February 2 (note the French soldier with the looted StG44 assault rifle).*

5 *Colmar Pocket memorial at Jebsheim. Angel3/WikiCommons*

6 *75th Division at Riedwihr on January 31.*

Left: *The Colmar Pocket survived for longer than could have been expected. Eisenhower blamed the French, but himself contributed to its longevity by halting Devers' eastern/northeast attacks and forcing him north in December. There was another reason: Alsace-Lorraine had become German as a result of the Franco-Prussian war of 1871 and had changed hands again in 1918. Hitler didn't want to lose his foothold in Alsace and was prepared to do as much as possible to retain the territory.*

Below: *12th Armored light tank at Rouffach on February 5. Rouffach is where the two task forces—American from the north, French I Corps from the south—met early on the 5th.*

On December 9, 1944, US 79th Infantry Division took Oberhoffen. The Germans, knowing that they were about to retreat, cleared the village of everything usable: all the goods in depots, factories, and shops went to the Reich. The cattle—183 of them—were requisitioned and the villagers had to lead them beyond the Rhine, as far as Ottersdorf near Rastatt. The village's best horses were also taken, as was food and industrial products. On December 6, the Kreisleiter in charge of the area forced men into the Volkssturm—the militia—and the families of those who did not show up were threatened with reprisals until they did. But as with so many places in Alsace, even this wasn't the end of the village's war. The Germans returned in the form of the 10. SS-Panzer Division Frundsberg on January 25, after the US 314th Infantry Regiment had retreated behind the River Moder. The Germans held Oberhoffen until the end of Operation Nordwind (February), when the Allies retook it. The German defensive Anne-Marie line—the front line in Alsace—now ran along the Haguenau–Schirrheim railroad line, south of Haguenau Forest, and Oberhoffen military camp was a significant German strong-point, protected by minefields. Facing it on March 16 was French First Army's 3e DIA, which—as part of Operation Undertone—was ordered to advance towards the German border. On March 15, 4e RTT and 3e RTA assaulted the positions held by 477. VGD, and captured Oberhoffen Camp on the 16th. What was left of the village and its area—fought over three times—was now free.

1 *Oberhoffen village is once again in American hands, February 3, 1945.*

2 *Children play with weapons left behind when the Germans fled in February 1945—including Kar98s and StG44s.*

3 *Pvt Kenneth G Walker of F/142 Infantry Regiment (36th Division) inspects the Jagdpanzer 38 he knocked out with a bazooka on February 13.*

4 *Memorial to 3e DIA, FR First and US Seventh armies in Oberhoffen.*

5 *25th Tank Bn, 14th Armored Division in Oberhoffen, February 6.*

The Maginot Line

Built by the French in the 1930s, the Maginot Line was designed to protect the new Franco-German borders following the Treaty of Versailles—and that included Alsace-Lorraine. The defensive line included gros and petit ouvrages (GO/PO—large and small forts), blockhouses and casemates armed with machine guns, mortars, howitzers, and flame-throwers often linked by underground passage-ways and protected by cleverly landscaped walls, fossé (moats or ditches), and armored embrasures cloches, or turrets. A formidable obstacle, it was bypassed in 1940 but came very much into play at the end of 1944 and in 1945. In December 1944, US Third and Seventh came up against it, the latter around the RF (région fortifée) de la Lauter—in particular Bitche and the gros ouvrages of Simer-shof, Schiesseck, Otterbiel, and Grand-Hohékirkel. It took the 398th Infantry (44th Division) a week to pacify GO Schiesseck and involved P-47 fighter-bombers, M12 155mm SP guns, 105mm-armed M4s, and the full weight of XV Corps' artillery.

Above Right: The 44th Division's 71st Infantry Regiment, with backup from the M36s of A/776th TD Battalion, assaulted GO Simserhof on December 14 and 15. This is Simserserhof Block 5 after the battle. L. Sertelet/CRT Lorraine

Right and Below: Two M8s of 92nd Cavalry Recon Squadron, 12th Armored Division, along with an M3A1 halftrack, at a captured Maginot petit ouvrage outside Rohrbach-lès-Bitche, on December 13. Today, "Fort Casso" is an excellent museum with a complete mixed arms turret in working condition.

Ever had that feeling of déjà vu? The 100th Infantry Division must have done as it returned to the Bitche area in March 1945. Having taken GO Schiesseck in December 1944, the 100th was attacked but held firm against 17. SS-Panzergrenadier Division during Operation Nordwind, and then had to retake ground—including a number of Maginot Line bunkers and GOs—lost during the German March 1945 offensive. They didn't take as long to clear out as in December—partly because of the demolitions carried out by both sides during and after the original fighting—and Bitche fell on March 16.

Above: Dead Jagdpanzer 38 and crew near Camp de Bitche, which was captured by XV Corps on March 17, 1945.

Right: M4A3E8 of 781st Tank Battalion, attached to 100th Division, enters Bitche, on March 16 as part of Operation Undertone. Note all five crew visible, heavy sandbag protection, 76mm gun, and HVSS.

8 REMEMBRANCE

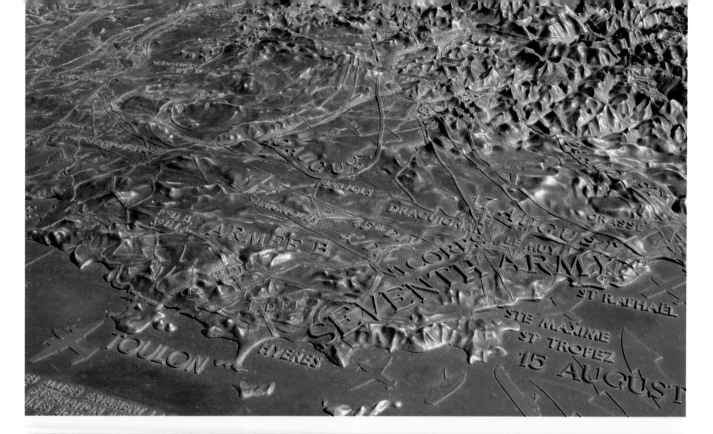

Previous Page: *The Rhône American Cemetery and Memorial, Draguignan was designed by Henry J. Toombs and A.F. Brinckerhoff. The sculpture of the Angel of Peace nurturing the new genertion was designed by Edmund Amateis and carved by Georges Granger. The cemetery holds 861 American dead.*

Above: *The bronze relief map at the cemetery was made by Bruno Bearzi of Florence. It's 20ft long by 11ft wide and extremely impressive.*

There are many memorials to the events of and troops who fought in the battles from the Riviera to the Rhine. The French involvement—First Army, the Resistance, the Armée Noire— is identified by many plaques, gravestones, statues, tanks, and memorials. The US side is also well-remembered not just in the magnificent and peaceful official cemeteries, but in street names and monuments in villages and towns throughout eastern France.

The casualties for the three campaigns—Riviera, Vosges, Nordwind—were substantial, although the landings themselves were, thankfully, astonishingly light: 95 dead and 385 wounded. In the month it took Seventh Army to reach the Vosges, US forces suffered over 15,000 casualties including some 7,300 dead. The French casualties were higher—4,500 in the taking of the ports alone. German casualties were nearly 160,000 including 7,000 dead and over 130,000 captured. Additionally, it's difficult to put a figure on the number of civilian casualties or those of the FFI. These figures give a feeling for the casualty levels:

Army	Killed	Wounded	Missing/ Captured	Total
US Seventh	1,383	8,373	1,256	11,012
FR First	1,719	6,899	291	8,909
Sixth AG Nov	3,102	15,272	1,538	19,921
US Seventh	1,619	8,328	1,856	11,803
FR First	1,820	8,884	1,073	11,777
Sixth AG Dec	3,439	17,212	2,929	23,580
US Seventh	1,877	8,907	4,837	15,621
FR First	1,475	7,289	1,539	10,303
Sixth AG Jan	3,352	16,196	6,376	25,924
TOTAL	9,893	48,680	10,843	69,425
German Army Jan 45				39,000

There are a number of national cemeteries and memorials to the dead along Seventh Army's route: Traces of War is an excellent online source for these.

Above: *Mosaic inside the chapel of the American Cemetery at Épinal.* Zairon/WikiCommons (CC BY-SA 4.0)

Left: *The Nécropole nationale de Sigolsheim holds 1,589 graves of French soldiers—mainly from the Alsace campaign. These are a few of the nearly 900 headstones to the African soldiers who died serving France.* Renardeau/WikiCommons (CC BY-SA 2.0)

Below: *Monument at the top of Mont de Sigolsheim honors the American soldiers who fought for the liberation of Alsace at the site of the battle of Sigolsheim in December 1944.* Lionel Allorge/ WikiCommons (CC BY-SA 3.0)

Opposite, Above and Center: *The German cemetery at Niederbronn-les-Bains holds 15,500 German war dead.*

Opposite, Below Left and Right: *Memorial to 1DFL on Illhaeusern church in the shape of the Cross of Lorraine.*

Above: *One of the kilometer markers that follows the path of 2DB from Normandy to Strasbourg. This one is at Grussenheim.*

Above Right: *Draguignan memorial to the Resistance in Var.*

Center Right: *Colmar memorial to the combatants of the 5DB on February 2, 1945.*

Below Right: *Memorial to 8RCA remembering the 121 dead in the area of Grussenheim at the end of January 1945.*

Below: *Memorial to American armor crossing the Moder canal on March 16, 1945, and offensive that freed Haguenau.*

ACKNOWLEDGMENTS

As always, loads of people helped with this book—in particular I'd like to thank my brother Jonathan, who wrote much of the introduction, the Armée d'Afrique piece, and biography of de Lattre. Thanks, too, to Leo Marriott who organized the trips to College Park and Neil Powell of *www.battlefield historian. com* who supplied photos; the brilliant website *Tracesof-war.com* which catalogs military memorials, monuments, museums, and fortifications and is essential if you want to plan visits, and the helpful staff of NARA at College Park, MD. Thanks also to Mark Franklin for the maps, Elly for design, and Sandra for navigating and keeping me company in France.

The information for the maps came from various sources. Most are based on the US official maps in the Clarke & Smith "Green Book" which can be found online at the US Army Center of Military History. Others were informed by the books and articles cited below in particular Breuer, De Lattre, Ganz (for the style and overall content of the map on p. 20), Gaujac, and Zaloga. The map on p. 9 is from the online resources of the University of Texas, Perry-Castañeda Library Map Collection collection. The map on p. 33 came from Hewitt; those on pp. 34–35, 37 were drawn by 19 Field Survey Co, RE. Those on pp. 126 and 129 are based on material from the Texas Military Forces Museum.

The unit artwork came from Noclador/WikiCommons (pp. 10, 11), MrInfo2012/ WikiCommons (p. 12), Marco Kaiser/Wikicommons (p. 21), Zscout370/WikiCommons (p. 26), US Army Institute of Heraldry/WikiCommons (p. 120), Steven Williamson/ WikiCommons (p. 124).

The photos also come from various sources. Modern images are mainly by the author or as credited otherwise. The wartime shots are mainly from NARA, Battlefieldhistorian, and the George Forty Collection. The following are from Getty Images (thanks to Chris Fortune for his help): 76C & B, 171 #6—Keystone-France/Gamma-Rapho; 93BL—Photo12/UIG; 139A & L—AFP; 164/165 credit on photo; 171 #5 & #7—Roger Viollet.

Thanks also to the following: Tourisme Lorraine for permission to use the bunker photo on p. 182; *http://www.45thdivision.org* for permission to use the Gerard Hall photos on p. 137; MOSSOT/WikiCommons (p. 29 inset below); R. Bruce Overman (inset images on p. 51); Villa La Begude (Patch memorial p. 70); US Mint (p. 160 Nisei Gold Medal); and Ji-Elle (Haut Jacques monument p. 162). Apologies if I've missed anyone.

Other helpful sites are:
• Lonesentry.com ("GI Stories" and other official pamphlets
• *http://www.history.army.mil* (the US Center of Military History is a wonderful location for the official histories and much more)
• *http://www.texasmilitary-forcesmuseum.org* (for info about the 36th Infantry Division) and *www.45thdivision.org* (info about the 45th)
• *https://forum.axishistory.com/* (for intelligent discussion and a huge base of knowledge on the Axis powers)
• Warfare History Network (some really excellent articles)
• *http://2db.forumactif.com* (info on Leclerc's 2e Division Blindée)
• *www.navsource.org* (everything you've ever wanted to know about US Navy vessels)
• US Militaria Forum (in particular the postings of Dogface 44)

BIBLIOGRAPHY

After the Battle magazine: *Number 110: The Riviera Landings*; After the Battle, 2000.

Airborne Missions in the Mediterranean 1942–1945; Air Force Historical Research Agency, USAF Historical Division, 1955.

Beard, Maj Rebecca E.: *Footnote in History: Sixth Army Group Operations in the Second World War and Lessons for Contemporary Planners*; Fort Leavenworth, 2016.

Bradley, Omar: *A Soldier's Story*; Henry Holt 1951.

Breuer, William B.: *Operation Dragoon The Allied Invasion of the South of France*; Airlife, 1987.

Clarke, Jeffrey J., and Smith, Robert Ross; United States Army in WWII The European Theater of Operations *Riviera to the Rhine*; CMH, 1993.

De Lattre, Marshal: *The History of the First French Army*; Allen & Unwin, 1952.

Dworak, David D.: *Victory's Foundation:US Logistical Support of the Army's Mediterranean Campaign, 1942–1945*; Syracuse University, 2011.

Ganz, A. Harding: *The 11th Panzers in the Defense, 1944*; Armor magazine, 1994.

Gassend, Jean-Loup: *Operation Dragoon Autopsy of a Battle*; Schiffer, 2013.

Gaujac, Paul: *Dragoon The Other Invasion of France*; Histoire & Collections, 2004.

Hewitt, Vice Adm H.K.: *Invasion of Southern France Report of Naval Commander, Western Task Force*; 1944.

Kaufmann, J.E. and H.W.: *Fortress France*; Stackpole, 2006.

Kaufmann, J.E. and H.W.: *The Maginot Line History and Guide*; Pen & Sword, 2011.

Moore, William Mortimer: *Free France's Lion The Life of Philippe Leclerc, De Gaulle's Greatest General*; Casemate, 2011.

Quigley, Maj Michael T.: *Operation Dragoon: The Race Up the Rhone*; Fort Leavenworth, 2016.

Rhône American Cemetery and Memorial; The American Battle Monuments Commission.

Various authors: *CSI Battlebook Operation Anvil/Dragoon*; Combat Studies Institute, 1985.

Volpe, Michael: Task Force Butler: *A Case Study in the Employment of an Ad Hoc Unit in Combat Operations*; 2007.

Whitlock, Flint: *Operation Nordwind: The "Other" Battle of the Bulge*; Warfare History, 2017.

Zaloga, Steven J.: Campaign 210 *Operation Dragoon 1944 France's Other D-Day*; Osprey, 2009.

Zaloga, Steven J.: New Vanguard 231 *Railway Guns of World War II*; Osprey, 2009.

Zaloga, Steven J.: Fortress 109 *The Atlantic Wall (3) The Südwall*; Osprey, 2009.

ABBREVIATIONS

1AATF	1st Airborne Assault Task Force		MACAF	Mediterranean Allied Coastal Air Forces
1/2/5DB	*1ère/2e/5e Division Blindée* (armored)		MASAF	Mediterranean Allied Strategic Air Forces
1DFL	*1re Division Française Libre (or DMI)*		MATAF	Mediterranean Allied Tactical Air Forces
1SSF	1st Special Service Force		NATOUSA	North African Theater of operations, US Army
2DIM	*2e Division d'Infanterie Marocaine* (Moroccan)		OBW	*Oberbefehlshaber West* (Commander-in-chief West)
3DIA	*3e Division d'Infanterie Algérienne*		OKH	*Oberkommando der Heeres* German Army
4DMM	*4e Division de Marocaine de Montagne*		High	
9DIC	*9e Division d'Infanterie Coloniale*			Command (Hitler)
AFAT	*Auxiliare Feminin de l'Arméede Terre*		PFAB	Parachute Field Artillery Battalion
BIMP	*Bataillon d'Infanterie de Marine du Pacifique*		PIB	Parachute Infantry Battalion
CC	Combat Command		PIR	Parachute Infantry Regiment
CG	Commanding general		PzGr	Panzergrenadier (armored infantry)
DD	Duplex drive		QF	Quick firing
DMI	*Division de Marche d'Infanterie*		RC	*Régiment de Chasseurs*
FFI	*Forces Françaises de l'Interieure*		RCA	*Régiment de Chasseurs d'Afrique*
FJR(6)	Fallschirmjäger (paratroops; FJR6 = 6th Regiment		RCC	*Régiment de Chars de Combat* (armored regt)
G/HMC	Gun/howitzer motor carria)ge		RCT	*Regimental Combat Team*
GTM	*Groupe de Tabors Marocaine*		RTA	*Régiment de Tirailleurs Algériens*
HKAA/R	*Heeres Küsten Artillerie Abteilung/Regiment*		RTM	*Régiment de Tirailleurs Marocains*
LCI	Landing craft, infantry		SHAEF	Supreme HQ Allied Expeditionary Force
LCM	Landing craft, mechanized		TAC	Tactical Air Command
LCT	Landing craft, Tank		TD	Tank destroyer
LCVP	Landing craft, vehicle/personnel		TF	Task Force
LE	*Legion Étrangère* (Foreign Legion)		VGD	*Volksgrenadier Division*
MAAF	Mediterranean Allied Air Forces			

INDEX